SEEING IT THROUGH

SEEING IT THROUGH

BY

TONY CONIGLIARO

WITH JACK ZANGER

THE MACMILLAN COMPANY

COLLIER-MACMILLAN LTD., LONDON

The Macmillan Company
866 Third Avenue, New York, N.Y. 10022
Collier-Macmillan Canada Ltd.,
Toronto, Ontario

Library of Congress Catalog Card Number:
72-124869

First Printing

Printed in the United States of America

It was only natural for me to team up with Jack Zanger when I decided to tell the story that is in this book. Jack had followed me through spring training one year for a story which appeared in a national magazine. As we worked on that story I got to know him well.

He knew how to make me think and talk. He knew how to reach my feelings and make them come out. With Jack at my side I learned things about myself—and in learning I grew.

I also learned about Jack. I came to know the depth of his feelings and the honesty he had about everything. Working closely with Jack, I also got to meet his wife Brenda and his year-old daughter Nora. I found out things about them but mostly how much they love Jack.

His last words to me were "See you in New York on Opening Day." He never made it. He never saw this book in print. Just days after completing the manuscript Jack died without a hint that at the age of forty-three he had no more time.

This is my story. But it is Jack Zanger's book. He was more than a writer. He was a very special man. Brenda and Nora and I will always know that.

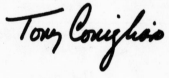

PART I

This book begins on August 18, 1967. I picked that date because it happens to be the whole reason for writing the book in the first place. I was hit in the head by a baseball, which nearly ended my career. It also nearly ended my life. A couple of inches higher and I'd be dead today. But by some miracle I'm not; in fact, I'm back playing baseball again. I wish to God that day never happened; why didn't it rain or something and wash out the ballgame? But it did happen, and because it did, it forced me to stop and think about myself for the first time in my life. Until then my life had been one long mad dash at making good in baseball. I'm not knocking it because I love baseball more than anything in the world. Anything. But whatever else was happening to me, I certainly wasn't aware of it. I don't know when or if I would have stopped to take stock of myself if that ball hadn't slammed into me and made me stop. If there was anything good about it, that was it.

We were playing a night game with the California Angels and

Fenway Park was packed the way it was for nearly all our home games in 1967. *We* were the Boston Red Sox and were fighting for a pennant. The last time the Red Sox had won a pennant was 1946, when I was one year old—one of the few times in my life I didn't think about becoming a major-league ballplayer. Just before I came to bat in the fourth inning, somebody threw a smoke bomb down on the field. A cloud of black smoke hung over the field, delaying the game about ten minutes. I'm not terribly superstitious, so I didn't think much about it. But I've thought about it a lot since then.

Jack Hamilton was pitching for the Angels. He was a hard thrower who was frequently accused of throwing spitballs, or greaseballs, or whatever you want to call them. The point is his ball broke in a funny way like no breaking pitch is supposed to break. He also has been known to throw at hitters. I had singled off a curve ball my first time up, so this time I went up there looking for a fastball. I made up my mind to try and hit it up the middle, hard. Just before he made his first pitch, I wondered if the delay had cooled him off, caused his arm to stiffen up. It was the last thought I had before he hit me.

The ball came sailing right toward my chin. Normally, a hitter can just jerk his head back a fraction and the ball will buzz right by. But this pitch seemed to follow me in. I know I didn't freeze, I definitely made a move to get out of the way of the ball. In fact, I jerked my head back so hard that my helmet flipped off just before impact.

Funny, you never go up there thinking you're going to be hit, and then in a fraction of second you know it's going to happen. When the ball was about four feet from my head I knew it was going to get me. And I knew it was going to hurt because Hamilton was such a hard thrower. I was frightened. I threw my hands up in front of my face and saw the ball follow me back and hit me square in the left side of the head. As soon as it crunched into me, it felt as if the ball would go in my head and come out the other side; my legs gave way and I went down like a sack of potatoes. Just before everything went dark I saw the ball bounce straight down on home plate. It was the last thing I saw for several days.

I was never knocked out but I wish I had been. I rolled on the ground trying to stop the pain in my head with my hands. The impact of the ball made both my eyes slam shut and I felt a tremendous swelling in my mouth. I couldn't see. I remember saying, *I'm blind, I can't see,* I remember saying that. Then I heard Rico Petrocelli's voice saying, "Take it easy, Tony. You're gonna be all right." Rico was the next hitter after me and he was the first person to reach me after I went down.

The swelling was so bad inside my mouth that I was worried about breathing. My mouth was filling up fast with fluid—I thought it was blood, but it wasn't, thank God. I had only a small opening that I could breathe through, and then the thought started running through my mind, *Suppose this thing closes up? I won't be able to breathe.* I thought, *Oh, Jesus, if this thing closes up on me, I'm gone.* That's when I asked God to keep me alive. That's when I knew He could take me if He wanted to. It was like a showdown between me and God, and I was afraid I would die right then and there.

If there was any sound coming from the stands, the pain in my head blotted it out. There was just one big deafening whistling going on inside my head. I couldn't see out of my eyes. I couldn't stand the pain and I couldn't do anything about it, and I immediately became sick to my stomach. Then I remembered that my family was in the stands, my mother and father and my two brothers, Billy and Richie. I didn't want them to worry and yet I knew they had to be worried by what they saw. I knew things looked terrible with me lying there on the ground. Later on, some of my teammates told me they thought I was dead. "Your eye looked crushed," Rico told me. "It made me sick to look at it."

I could make out Buddy LeRoux's voice telling me to lie still until the stretcher came. Buddy was the club's trainer and I had always felt close to him. Then, after what seemed like a year of waiting, I felt myself being lifted onto a stretcher and I was carried off the field and into the clubhouse. They stretched me out on one of the trainer's tables and Buddy put an ice pack against the side of my head. "Buddy, this pain is killing me," I said. "Give me something." It hurt so much I could hardly talk.

"I can't Tony," he said. "Just relax. Dr. Tierney's right here."

The Red Sox team physician, Dr. Thomas M. Tierney, had been sitting in the stands, and the moment he saw them carry me off he rushed down and was waiting for me in the clubhouse when I got there. He's been a close friend of my family for years and knowing he was in the picture made me feel a little better. But when he didn't say anything to me and just acted like a doctor, I became worried about my condition all over again. What he did, while waiting for an ambulance to come—though I didn't know it at the time—was to test my blood pressure and reflexes.

I had no idea what was happening to me and I just felt helpless. The room was deathly quiet. If I hadn't heard the scraping of spikes on the hard floor I would have thought there was something wrong with my ears, too. Some of my teammates had come back from the dugout to see how I was. A couple of guys grabbed my wrist and squeezed hard to encourage me, but nobody was saying anything. I don't know how many of them came back or even who they were, but it was very reassuring. But I know that

Dick Williams never came back and that's always bothered me. Maybe he was too busy at the time, but the fact is that he never let me feel warm about him afterward—not that it ever was that way between us before.

Somehow, I knew my father was there, even though he didn't say a single word. Buddy LeRoux told me later how easy my father made it for everybody by just standing there off to one side, keeping out of the way and not making a scene. We're a very close family, very emotional, and in times of trouble we really come together. But my father is also blessed with a special calm that comes over him in situations where he knows there's nothing he can do, and I'll never know how he kept himself under control that night. Billy and Richie had come into the clubhouse with him and I found out later that Richie had hidden in a corner and bawled into the wall so that I wouldn't hear him.

Outside somewhere, I heard the wailing of an ambulance siren. I thought, *Thank God, now maybe I'll get something to kill this pain.* By now, I just felt like screaming out and crying, but I didn't want to act like a baby in front of my father and brothers. I was trying to hold it all in, but it was very hard for me to remain quiet and just lie there. If I could have had just one wish then, it would have been for the pain to go away. Believe me, I didn't think about my baseball career or if I'd ever play again. At this moment I just wanted to be alive. I realized how much my life meant to me.

When I was carried out of the clubhouse, there were a lot of people milling around at the entrance, and I could hear them calling to me, saying things like, "Hang in there, Tony," and "You'll be back soon, kid." It would have been beautiful if only I could have appreciated it then. But I was just in misery and wanted out. The ride to the hospital was the longest ride of my life, even though it was only about fifteen minutes from Fenway Park. The driver was speeding all the way with the siren going full blast, and every time he turned a corner or put on the brakes I thought my head would split wide open. My father and Dr. Tierney rode with me in the back.

I was taken to Sancta Maria Hospital in Cambridge, just across the Charles River. Once I got there I thought they'd stop the pain. But the first thing they did was bring me to an examination room where a neurosurgeon looked me over and took X-rays. They were afraid I might be hemorrhaging internally. I wasn't, but if I had been I would have been in real trouble. Every time they moved the position of my head to take a picture I felt like screaming at them to get the hell out of there and leave me alone. But I knew I had to hang on. The pain was so severe now that even if I could see out of my eyes it would have hurt too much to open them.

Finally, I was taken upstairs to a room and put in bed. I was extremely woozy and just wanted to sleep; but I couldn't because the pain was still with me, worse than ever. Fluid was oozing out of my mouth onto the pillow—I still thought it was blood. My parents were allowed to come in for a few minutes with Billy and Richie. They didn't say very much. My mother just held my hand, trying not to cry. But she is a woman with great feelings, and unlike my father, she shows them most of the time. I didn't want to make things worse by telling her how much my head hurt and it killed me to know how miserable everyone was. I silently asked God not to let this thing tear them up and make any of them sick because of me.

After they left, the thought shot through me that I might never see them again. Death was constantly on my mind and I still felt I had a good chance of dying. I had hoped the doctors would knock me out but they didn't. So, lying there in the dark trying to sleep with all those terrible thoughts, an empty feeling came over me. I wanted to have someone around to hold onto, but no one was there now. I was never so alone in my whole life.

During the night I managed to sleep in spurts of fifteen or twenty minutes at a time. Either I'd wake up with the pain running through my head, or it was the nurse coming to check on me. Sancta Maria Hospital is a Catholic hospital and some of the nurses are nuns. My nurse would come in to take my pulse and blood pressure every fifteen minutes or so. Once I remember asking her, "Am I gonna be all right?" and she said, "Oh, you're fine. You'll be all right." You know the way they talk. But it frightened me to death the way she kept running out to find the doctor every time. In my whole life this was probably the closest I ever felt to God. I've never been terribly religious. Oh, I go to church on Sundays, but that's just because I grew up doing it. But now I was begging Him to let me live. I wasn't thinking of baseball anymore.

The next thing I remember was waking up the next morning and feeling someone holding my hand. A voice said, "It's me, Tony, Tom Yawkey." I couldn't believe it. Yes, I could. I'd believe anything about this fine man who owns the Red Sox. He had always been kind and patient with me and listened to my problems; I knew I could always go to him when I was in trouble, and I went to him many times. Now, as busy as he was, he was sitting here in my room, holding my hand, and telling me not to worry about anything.

I think I realized then that this was the guy I was really playing for, nobody else. Maybe I didn't like Dick Williams very much and griped about him, but this was the man who really mattered. Him and, of course, my family and my fans. Tom Yawkey is not only the best owner in baseball, he's the best friend a ballplayer ever had. He'd do anything to help his players; and he knows I'd do anything for him.

A little later my family showed up. I wasn't feeling much better than the night before. My head still pained, maybe not as bad, but it was still piercing my skull. My eyes were still closed. When I tried to open them, I found I couldn't get the left one open—that's how swollen it had become—and I could just about peek out of my right eye. All I saw was a blur and it was hard trying to keep it open.

Except for my family, I wasn't allowed any other visitors. But a couple of hours later I heard a commotion going on outside my room. The door was slightly open and I heard the nun say, "But you can't come in here. He's not having any visitors." Then I heard another voice say, "Ah, come on, Sister, just let me in for a minute." I recognized that voice, all right. It was Mike Ryan, my roommate and closest friend on the ballclub. "Is that you, Mike?" I called out.

"Hey, roomie, you in there?" he yelled. "Hey, come on out. I got the babes and some beer waiting downstairs in the car. Let's go." I thought the nun would have a fit. But I was too sick to even laugh. "No, I'm dying, Mike," I said. "Some other time."

"Come on, Sister," Mike said. "See, he needs me. Let me in." She finally did. "How'd you get up here, anyway?" I asked him. "Sneaked up through the fire escape," he laughed, and it made me laugh, too. He stayed a while and we talked, and when he left I felt a lot better than I did before he came. I also found out that Jack Hamilton had come by that morning and wanted to see me, but they wouldn't let him up.

There was absolutely nothing I could do those first couple of days in the hospital except lie there like a vegetable. But once I realized I was out of danger, I began thinking for the first time about the beaning. About Jack Hamilton. The big question I asked myself was did he hit me intentionally. I had been in a slight hitting slump going into the series with the Angels and pitchers don't usually try to stir guys up who are slumping. If I had been hot at the time, it would have been a different story. So I decided to give him the benefit of the doubt. Even though I knew he had a tendency to hit guys on occasion. I figured he had no good reason for going after me. Only one person in the whole world knows if Jack Hamilton was trying to hit me that night. That person is Jack Hamilton.

Besides, I figured the pitch he hit me with was a spitter. I was hit because of the crazy way it broke in on me. If a guy's going to hit you, or even brush you back, he certainly isn't going to throw a spitter in that situation. That's when he gives you smoke. I didn't feel one way or the other about Hamilton before he beaned me and I don't hate him for what he did, I have no grudge against him. But I wouldn't invite him over to the house for dinner, either.

It's not that I object to getting thrown at. That's part of baseball and I've always accepted it. I feel brushback pitches are part of the game, but not beanballs. There's a difference. It may be a slight difference, but it's there just the same. It's maybe a difference of a couple of inches, a difference between being hit and not being hit, a difference of what's on the pitcher's mind. Some pitchers intend to hit the batter. Some just try to loosen him up a little at the plate so he doesn't get a good toehold. I'll go along with that. But any pitcher who deliberately throws at a batter is a coward. It takes more guts to throw the ball over the plate.

When I woke up on my second morning in the hospital, I was the happiest guy in the world. I could see again. Not great, not with both eyes, but I could see. The sight of my right eye was fuzzy, but I could make things out. All I saw were flowers and

17

mail sacks, a roomful of them. But it was the mail that knocked me out. There were thousands of letters—when we counted them we found there were 13,000 of them—from people all over the country. I figured they must have started writing the night I was hurt.

The mail kept coming in every day after that, and then I started receiving rosary beads and other religious objects from people of many different faiths. I realized all the prayers that had been said for me and I honestly felt this was the main reason I was alive. I was grateful more than I could say and I kept telling myself that God pulled me through this and that in some way I would repay Him and all those people who didn't even know me for what they had done.

Just being able to see again revived my spirits. The left eye was still blown up and closed tight, and looking out of my right eye made everything seem like it was nighttime. I couldn't tell sunlight or whether it was a beautiful day outside or a cloudy one. The headaches eased off to where I could go a few hours without feeling any pain. *That's* when they started giving me all the medication I needed. That's when Dr. Tierney told me how bad things looked when I was first brought there.

"You're a lucky guy, Tony," he said. "We were really worried about you for the first twenty-four hours or so. Had the pitch been two inches higher, you would have been dead." He then explained that I had suffered a linear fracture of the left cheekbone and a dislocated jaw. I had taken the brunt of the pitch high up near my temple and the tremendous concussion is what caused my eye to slam shut. He told me that even after the eye opened it would be weeks before the swelling would go down so they could examine the damage inside. He's a real pro and I'm glad he always leveled with me.

But I had every reason to expect I'd still be playing ball again that season. And frankly, listening to the games on the radio made me itch to get back into the pennant race. I wasn't able to look at television because my right eye was still very sensitive to light, but I figured this would pass in a few days. My father read the papers to me where they were saying I'd be out four to six weeks, which practically meant the rest of the season. "What are they talking about?" I said. "They're crazy. I'll be back in the lineup in ten days. Just as soon as the eye opens."

On his next visit, Dr. Tierney asked me if I wanted to have a look at myself in the mirror. "Is it that bad?" I asked him. He held a mirror in front of me and what I saw in the reflection sickened me. The left eye was all black and purple and was about the size of a handball. When I looked close I could actually make out the imprint of the stitches where the ball had hit me. On top of that, I had lost seven or eight pounds and I looked pale and emaciated; and my face hadn't been shaved since the night of the beaning.

Because of the dislocated jaw, I hadn't been able to take any solid food. I couldn't chew so I drank my meals through a straw. I love ice cream and whenever my parents came up they'd bring me a frappe with eggs in it. But eventually I was able to eat pizza and I felt like I was back with the living. For the whole time I was in the hospital, Mr. Yawkey came to see me every day. So did a lot of my teammates, guys like Mike Ryan and Rico Petrocelli and George Scott. But I never heard from Dick Williams at all. He never came up to the hospital and he never dropped me a line or anything.

This upset me. I felt I had contributed something to the ball-club and had given the man everything I had. I had been hit in the face by a baseball and nearly lost my life, and I felt the least he could do was show he knew I existed. Sure, my relationship with Williams up to that time hadn't been a great one; we never were the best of friends. But I did my job. I played ball and didn't give him any trouble. I guess we just started out disliking each other and things never got any better. We first met back in 1964, when I was a rookie trying to make the ballclub and he was a veteran trying to hang on. Somehow, they roomed us together for a short time. We never got along. I didn't like him because he was cocky. Johnny Pesky was the manager then and he was always talking behind Pesky's back, saying how he would have done things differently. He acted like he knew it all and I couldn't understand what he had to be so cocky about when he never could hit a baseball very well in his whole life.

Time dragged on in the hospital. By the third day, the sight in my right eye came back pretty close to normal and the left eye opened slightly. It still looked as if I was in a dark room all the time. Being cooped up was beginning to bug me now, and I was worried about how long it would take for the eye to return to normal. The Red Sox had put me on the twenty-one-day disabled list, which meant I couldn't play anytime before September 9. But now I was beginning to realize it was going to be quite a battle getting back before the season was over. I felt this even more when, about ten days after I was hit, the Red Sox picked up Ken Harrelson, who had been released by the Athletics because he'd had some words with owner Charley Finley. They said they wanted Harrelson to give them some right-hand power and to play right field, even though his normal position is first base. So that told me something, too. The team wasn't so sure I'd be back in time.

I didn't resent them picking up Harrelson. Anytime you get a guy with his home-run bat you're helping yourself offensively. But I felt cheated and angry because of what I was missing out on. We were going for a pennant and there is absolutely nothing like it in the world when it's happening to you. You forget about petty grievances or who you like or you don't like; you're all in the same thing together, and it's a great feeling. This club had such youth and spirit and desire that it was wonderful being around these men. It was a pleasure going to the park every day, and I even enjoyed having the writers around. Every game was a big one and we were all too excited to be tired. I wanted to get back to all this, but every time I asked Dr. Tierney when my eye would clear up he would tell me that same thing. "It takes time, Tony. I don't really know." But time was running out on me, and so was the season.

It got especially bad listening to the games on the radio. The night I was hit we were in third place, about two and a half games behind the Twins. The White Sox and Tigers were right in there, too, and the standings would change almost every day. One day the nurse turned the radio on for me and the Red Sox were losing, 8–0. I fell asleep while the game was still on, but when I woke up I found out we had won, 9–8. That really made my day and showed everybody the kind of club we had. Winning games like that boosts a club's confidence in itself, where they know that being 4 or 5 runs behind doesn't mean a thing. You can always come back, you tell yourself, and you believe it. This team did and it gave the guys added drive. While I was in the hospital they went on a seven-game winning streak and were just two percentage points out of first place. If I was only back with them, I knew I could help them go the rest of the way.

At the time of my beaning I was having what was probably my best all-around year. I was hitting .287 and had twenty homers and knocked in sixty-seven runs. The only time I had ever hit for a higher average in the majors was my rookie year of 1964, when I batted .290. The next year I was the American League's home-run champion with 32 and at twenty became the youngest player ever to lead the league in homers. The way I was hitting the ball in 1967 I think I could have come close to .290 again and finished with about 30 homers and 100 RBI's. When I first made the majors, I set three goals for myself: I wanted to bat over .300, hit at least 30 homers and drive in 100 or more runs in a season. That might have been a little out of my reach in '67, but I was closing in on it.

I think every girl I ever went out with wrote me while I was in the hospital, and I don't know how many people tried to get in to see me, but they just weren't allowing visitors, except for my family and some close friends like my teammates. The mail kept pouring in and my mother read me some of the letters. But it wasn't till maybe six or seven months later that I found out who really wrote me because it took us all that time to go through the mail. Most of the people who wrote had never met me, yet they sounded as if they knew me anyway. They wrote very touching letters, telling me how terrible they felt about my being hurt and encouraging me not to give up. There were prayers in them and not just from Catholics; I think people of every religion wrote me.

I know being in the public eye always brings a lot of fan mail, but usually this is when you're going good and people want to share in it. The fact they wanted to communicate with me when I was down made me feel even better than I did in the good times. But I honestly wasn't paying much attention to the mail while I was in the hospital. I was locked up with other thoughts like getting out of there, wishing the damned eye would open up, and playing ball again. I didn't even think about girls.

The last day I was in the hospital, a Dr. I. Francis Gregory came to see me. He was the ophthalmologist at Sancta Maria and Dr. Tierney had asked him to look at my eye. He was a nice little man and he kept calling me "my boy" all the time. Anyway, he ran some tests on my left eye and told me I was 20/80, which wasn't too bad considering how recently I had been hit. My right eye was 20/15 and they concluded that my left eye must have been about the same before the injury.

"I'd like to run some more tests on you while you're in here," Dr. Gregory told me. I shook my head. "No, I have to get away from here," I said. "I'm going nuts. I want to get away for a little vacation." He said he guessed that would be all right, if that's what I wanted to do. He didn't think it would do me any harm. "But when you get back, I'd like you to come see me at my office." I let out a deep sigh to show what I thought of that. But I agreed, and he gave me his address in Cambridge. At least I was getting out of the hospital. Now I'd be able to eat some home cooking and build my strength back up. I was still pretty weak, and my appetite hadn't been too good in the hospital.

The Red Sox paid all the hospital bills. I'm sure they didn't have to pay every dime of it, but they did. To my mind, that team is the greatest baseball organization in both leagues. They'd always shown they cared about me and have given me everything I wanted. Except for my first year with them I've never had to battle with them at contract time. So when I walked out of that hospital free and clear I was well aware of the kind of class operation they run.

When it came time to leave we didn't want to make any kind of dramatic exit. I just wanted to get away with as little publicity as possible. So we asked the people at the hospital to keep it quiet.

23

They did their best, but still, there were four photographers waiting outside when we left. The Boston papers had been calling
the hospital right along trying to find out when I was leaving.

My father came and got me with the car. My legs were pretty
steady since I had been taking little walks for the past couple of
days. But I wasn't ready for the bright sunlight I walked into. It
really blinded me. My left eye was open, barely, but I couldn't
see a thing out of it, and my right eye was still sensitive to the
light, which made me blink when I first got outside. On the ride
home I closed my eyes and dozed.

My family lives in Swampscott, which is on the north shore
about eleven miles above Boston. It's a nice quiet town that be-
comes a resort town in the summer. Even though I've had my own
apartment in Boston for several years, I still go back there quite
often and I really regard it as my home. To get to Swampscott you
first have to go through Revere and Lynn, and the ride almost
traces a straight line through the places where I've lived. Whenever I drive out to see my folks, I can see the house where I was
born in Revere and the first baseball field I ever played on. Sometimes, when I'm in a thoughtful mood, I remember things from
my boyhood.

The farther out of Boston you go, the nicer the towns get, the
less congested they are. Swampscott's a pretty nice place, quite
rural, with very nice and, in some cases, expensive houses. Since
1964 we've lived in a modern colonial house my father helped
design.

My father's not a rich man, but he's not a lazy one, either. The
reason we were eventually able to move to Swampscott is that he's
worked hard all his life and managed to save enough money so we
could live well. About a year ago, he began building his real
dream house on some land he's owned for a few years. It's not far

from Swampscott, way out on the water in a place called Nahant, and when it's finished it's going to be a real showplace. My father's worked at many jobs in his lifetime. Right now he's a plant manager at the Triangle Tool and Die Company in Lynn, Massachusetts. But he's had some tough times, too. He knows what it's like to be hard-up for money, but the thing that always bailed him out was that he was never afraid to take a chance. Some of his business schemes flopped, but at least he tried. One time, he got some chickens and planned to sell them at a profit, but they all got sick and died and he lost his money. Another time he and his brother Guy bought up a lot of Christmas trees and told themselves, boy, we're going to get rich selling them before the holidays. They stood on a street corner every day for weeks, but nobody would pay them what they were asking, so they had to bring their price down to sell any trees and they wound up making $3.85 and they both came down with pneumonia.

But the point is that my father is a pretty big man to me. He's always there when you need him. The family comes first with him. When I was a kid, if my mother called him and told him she was having trouble with me, he'd leave work no matter what time it was and come home to see about the problem. He handled it, usually with his hand. But he handled it. So when it came time for me to leave the hospital, who else but my father would be there to come and take me home?

The day after I got home my parents and I went away to Grossinger's for a vacation. Grossinger's is a year-round resort in the Catskills in New York State. We were invited there by Lou Goldstein, who is the social director there and a great guy. I met him in 1963 when I was in my first year in baseball at Wellsville, N.Y. We hit it off and he told me, "Tony, any time you want to

2 5

come up here as my guest, you let me know. That goes even if you never make the major leagues." Fortunately, I did make the major the next year and I've been a fan of Grossinger's ever since. It's a great place to be, surrounded by mountainous scenery. It's also a fine place to meet girls, since a lot of the young crowd is always up there, but believe me, girls weren't on my mind much just then. I needed a lot of rest and sleep, so I didn't go up there with my parents to do any serious chasing.

We stayed about twelve days. I ate all that good Jewish food to fatten me up, took a tennis lesson, but otherwise I stayed mostly to myself. I would sit alone outside and try closing my right eye to see what, if anything, I could see out of my left. It wasn't much and was terribly blurred. I'd feel a few tears come to my eyes and then I'd try not to think about it. One night I tried to go to the nightclub they have on the grounds but the smoke and lights bothered my eyes and I got a headache right away; so I stayed away from the nightclub.

While we were at Grossinger's I felt my eye improving, or at least I thought it was. But when I got home I could see very little change. Things looked double and I found that if I didn't want to do silly things like tipping over glasses, I'd have to reach for them slowly. There was still too much swelling on the inside of the eye for the doctors to examine me, but still I told myself that I'd somehow be back in the lineup before the season was over. Maybe I was covering up and was worried more than I admitted to myself.

When I got home, I phoned Dr. Gregory and we set up an appointment. The first thing he did when I got there was give me an ordinary eye test: looking at a chart. I could make out the big E on top with my left eye and not much else below it. He looked a little grim at this point and began poking around the eye with

2 6

a few instruments. Then he said, "This is not so good, my boy. Something's happened to the eye. It's grown worse since the last time I saw you. Something is seriously wrong with the seeing part of your eye. Look, let's go down to see my friend Charlie Regan at the Retina Associates. He's equiped to do things I can't do here. This is a retinal job and I want him to see it."

I felt weak all over. My throat stuck and I didn't know if I could talk. I was as scared as I've ever been in my life. I could tell the eye wasn't too good even before I came to see Dr. Gregory. But I had been telling myself that it was too early to see any improvement, that this was normal in such cases. It would begin to clear up. Now he was telling me things had gotten worse in the ten days or so since I'd seen him in the hospital, and this was the scary part. I finally managed to say, "What does this mean? Will it get better?"

"I can't tell you that now," Dr. Gregory said. "I think you might have a bleb on your eye, or to be precise, on your macula. That's where you get all your direct, central vision from. When the ball hit your cheekbone the bone gave way—something had to give from all that impact. The macula is the weakest part of your eye, and now I think you have a bleb on it that is causing all the trouble."

"Bleb? What's a bleb?" I said.

"That's slang for cyst," he said. "A blister, if you like. It's normal for one to form after an injury like the one you've just had. But I can't tell anything more until we get a closer look at it. That's why I suggested we go see Charley Regan. They're equipped for this kind of retinal thing down there."

The next day I met Dr. Gregory downtown at the Retina Associates. These are a group of eye doctors who work out of the Mass. Eye and Ear Clinic and practice together when they're not at the hospital. I found out that Dr. Regan was one of the leading ophthalmologists in the country. The building looked like an abandoned warehouse, located across the Charles Street Circle a couple of blocks from Mass. Eye and Ear. The whole thing was beginning to frighten me. It looked to me like I was being passed from doctor to doctor but none of them could tell me when or if I'd ever play ball again. Now I was at some clinic I never heard of with a whole staff of doctors who would look at me. I was getting into the big leagues in this thing and it scared me to death.

When we got inside I met Dr. Regan. Dr. Gregory told him about my case and Dr. Regan said he had heard about my being hit in the head the night it happened. Dr. Regan was a man probably about the same age as my father, with silvery brown hair and pretty distinguished looking. While they talked I got the uncomfortable feeling of being out of it. I mean I knew they were discussing my case, but it was in all those medical terms and they could have been discussing someone else for all I knew. Finally, Dr. Regan said, "Let's get on with it."

I guess that was the first time I met Miss Molly McCormick. She's a nurse on the staff and in time she was to become my best friend there. I was so jumpy and impatient and always trying to get it over with, but she was just great in calming me down and talking to me. First she gave me a standard eye test. It wasn't much better than the one I'd just taken in Dr. Gregory's office. I couldn't see past the first couple of lines with my left eye. My right eye was fine. Then Dr. Regan came over and told me he was going to anesthetize my eye. He put some drops in it and it was like the eye fell asleep a few moments later. This allowed him to get a good look inside the eye. I didn't know it then but he told me later he was testing the pressure of my eye to see if I was developing glaucoma, which sometimes happens after such a blow. Once he saw I didn't have glaucoma he put some more drops in my eye to dilate it. These gave him a real good look at the retina. I've never liked being in a doctor's office although I've been in my share of them all my life, so I was uneasy. I kept jiggling my feet. I did everything he asked but I couldn't wait to get out of there.

"Ah, I see it," Dr. Regan said.

"See what?" I asked.

"The edema," he said, still looking. "That's the swelling that resulted from the impact of the ball. It's formed by the fluid. But this is a fairly common occurrence in this type of injury. It's to be expected." Every time somebody looked in my eye, he nodded and said, "Oh, yes, very normal. You expect to see that in a case like yours." If I was so normal how come I couldn't see out of the eye?

After that I got a couple of visual field tests, where they put a black patch over my right eye and I tried to follow a light across a screen. Later, I took a distortion test, where I tried to trace these boxes while looking at them with only my left eye.

When it was all over I sat with Dr. Regan in his office and he tried to explain to me the condition of my left eye. He told me that I had a blind spot which was caused by the formation of a cyst which in turn was formed from the swelling. This blind spot was on the macula which is in the center of the retina. The macula itself is only about 1/10 of an inch in diameter, he explained, and the cyst was on top of that. But the macula is our source of vision, which enables us to read small, fine print; or, as Dr. Regan explained to me, lets me judge the speed and distance of a base-ball coming at ninety miles an hour. He told me that the blind spot impaired my distance judgment and that the vision in my left eye was 20/100.

29

I don't claim I understood everything he said then. It's clearer to me now looking back on it. But I do remember that it sounded terrible, bad, and that it was very hard to take. I figured out I was in serious trouble. What Dr. Regan sounded like to me was a man telling me why I wasn't able to play ball. That's what it amounted to in my mind and I felt completely empty inside. I was in a hurrry to get away from there, as though if I walked out into the street I'd find he was wrong and that my eye would be normal again. I was afraid to ask him any questions but I knew I must. "Will I ever be able to see well enough to play ball again?" I tried to make it sound as flip as I could, like I really didn't care what his answer was. But I was almost afraid to hear his answer.

"I don't know," he said as nicely as he could. "The eye may still be undergoing changes. It's only been four weeks since you were hit. It may be healing. It's something we'll have to watch for a while. I want you to come back next week." I grunted and said okay.

A couple of days after we got home I found Richie marching around the house wearing his baseball glove. It was unusual for Richie to be in the house. He's a great athlete and I've always felt he's probably going to sign for some kind of record bonus when he graduates from high school in June of 1970. There he was with his glove and ball, so I said, "Hey, Richie, toss me the ball."

He did and we started up a small game of catch in the house and after a while I suggested we go outside and have a real catch. "Wait'll I get another glove," I told him. In the back of mind I wanted to see if I would have any trouble seeing the ball. We have a pretty good-sized backyard at home so we could stand pretty far apart and really fire the ball. When Richie threw me the ball I noticed right away it wasn't the way it used to be. I found I had to concentrate very hard on watching the ball with my right eye or I'd catch it in the heel of my glove.

I could tell Richie was watching me closely. He'd never say anything, of course, but I knew what he was thinking. Look, he admires me—that's what he was hanging around the house for in the first place. He was always around me even before I was hurt. If I came home he'd be there. When I wasn't home my mother couldn't find him even at supper time. But I didn't want to worry him, so I started fooling around. "Hey, Richie," I called out, "watch this curve." And I started breaking off curve balls. I used to pitch when I was in high school, so I began making like a pitcher. And before long I was really firing them in. That may have been the first time I ever even thought I might some day have to try to make it back as a pitcher, though I can't say I consciously thought about it then.

"Hey," Richie yelled out, "if you're gonna throw that hard, let me get a catcher's mitt." When he returned he found me building a little mound out there. "You'll ruin dad's lawn," he told me. But I didn't care, and I said, "Come on, help me." We made a mound and then I really began burning them in. I could follow through all right and put the ball where I wanted to, but it was hard to see the ball clearly when Richie threw it back to me. I tried to be nonchalant, flick out my glove at the last second to make the catch. That way, I thought, if I dropped a throw, it wouldn't look so bad. It would look accidental. I don't know if he caught on, but Richie kept his mouth shut.

Afterward, I suggested a game of pepper. Richie got a bat and began throwing the ball in and I'd rap it back at him. Or tried to. It wasn't the same either. I guess I got my bat on the ball most of the time but I missed a couple. That may not seem like much, but I never missed hitting the ball in pepper in my whole life.

Never. This was the first time. All Richie did was laugh and keep tossing the ball in. Once, when I rapped one pretty hard, he said, "Hey, you're better with one eye than I am with two." Then I knew he was thinking. But neither of us said anything.

Finally, I was so disgusted with myself I said, "That's enough." I went into the house and straight to my room. I holed up in my room just thinking about it and finally dropped off to sleep. But the next day I was out there with Richie trying again. There was no change. I kept fouling off a few or missing the ball completely. One time I remember throwing the bat against the fence and running inside the house. I now realized that if things didn't improve in a hurry there'd be no chance I'd be back playing ball that year.

I had been staying away from the ballpark because I didn't think I could stand going there and not being able to play, but finally I went back. This was about four weeks after I was hit. I got to Fenway early before the guys went out to take batting practice. When I opened the clubhouse door everything looked the same. The guys were still dressing, some of them standing near their lockers wearing their shirts and baseball hose, but no pants, others catching up on their fan mail. Reggie Smith, our rookie centerfielder, was sitting against his locker smoking a cigarette, Carl Yastrzemski was on the trainer's table getting some hot stuff put on his arm, George Scott was looking over a pile of bats trying to pick the ones with hits in them.

They all seemed to see me at once. But there was a split second before anybody made a move toward me; I had caught them by surprise, I could see that. Then they were all over me, crowding around, Rico and Scotty and Mike Ryan. "Hey, kid," Rico said. "How ya doing? Gee, you look great."

"Whatya say, roomie?" Mike Ryan said. "Come down to give the troops a pep talk?"

"T.C., T.C.," Scotty said. "Hey, gimme five, man," and he slapped palms with me.

I was glad to see them, of course, but there was also a nervousness in me I couldn't explain either. Then Dick Williams walked out of his office and came up to me from the far end of the locker room. I have no recollection of what he said, though it must have been something like, "Hello, Tony, how do you feel?" He stuck out his hand and my immediate response was to stick mine out. I felt he did it because he had to. What else could he do? He was right there when I came in. But I don't remember what I said to him. I know I didn't say what was on my mind, which was, "Where the hell were you before this? Why couldn't you at least come to the hospital just once? Or write me or call me on the telephone?" I thought it but I didn't say it, of course. Not once, not then or at any other time did he ever say a word about it to me, and I knew exactly where he stood in my league.

I honestly can't say I really developed a hatred for the guy, but I lost a lot of respect for him then; my dislike came later. I don't care how busy he was, he could have taken the time to come see me. Or written me. Now he was acting like I hadn't even been hit. It was as though he just took it for granted I had come down to the ballpark. Maybe I expected too much, but I think he owed me something after I got hit in the head. Yet he didn't show me anything. I don't forget something like that.

Seeing Williams was the toughest part of going back to Fenway Park, and I kept telling myself I had gone back for the sake of the guys. But to tell you the truth, I felt like an outsider in that clubhouse then. It had been my home in baseball for four years, but now I felt like I didn't belong there. I wasn't able to contribute anything. I couldn't play and help them in the pennant drive; I was just a visitor. I felt all knotted up inside and I knew my guts would explode if I didn't get out of there in a hurry. So I made my excuses. "Look, I got to go now," I said. "This headache of mine keeps coming back. I can't stay for the game, but I'll watch you on television." I left a few minutes later. When I got home I didn't watch the game on television.

The next time I went back to Fenway Park I suited up. I had to feel a part of it, even if I wasn't. But I wouldn't take any hitting. I knew how bad I'd look because my eye wasn't any better and I felt I'd make a fool out of myself. So I went to the outfield to shag flies, but even out there I wasn't too sure of my vision. When the ball came at me I got a double image. I saw two or three baseballs coming at me at the same time, when I knew there was only one, so I decided not to try to catch any of them. I finessed it. I let the ball drop a few feet in front of me and then I'd nonchalantly pick it up. Some of the guys who were out there with me would ask, "How's the eye, Tony?" and I'd say, "Oh, fine. It's coming along real good." That's all I'd say. I didn't want to tell anybody my problems. They were going for a pennant and I didn't want them to have anything else on their minds. I didn't think it was right for them to worry about me.

A week after my first examination with Dr. Regan I went back there again. They started doing the whole thing over again. I read the eye chart and it was no worse than the last time—or no better. But when Dr. Regan wanted to dilate my eye again I told him I didn't want him to. He looked amazed, and asked me why not. I told him I didn't want him to do it, that's all. He didn't argue with me. I didn't tell him that I was planning to go to Fenway and work out. I knew if he dilated the eye it would be blurry for hours and I wouldn't be able to see the ball. I had to see how I'd be at the plate. After checking me over and seeing no change from last week he let me go and I made another appointment for the following week.

After I left Dr. Regan's office I drove out to Fenway Park. The club was on the road, but I knew the clubhouse boys would be there. They're around every day, even when the team is away, cleaning up the locker room, restocking supplies, straightening up after a home stand. They also show up because Mr. Yawkey comes every day to work out and they play pepper with him.

When I walked into the clubhouse Keith Rosenfield, our regular bat boy, was sanding down a bat. I didn't see Mr. Yawkey around so I figured he'd been there already and left. "Hey, Moe," I said, "I feel like working out today. How about flipping some into me?" I don't remember why but I always called him Moe. He's a small kid with big dark eyes and those eyes sure bugged out now. All the kids who worked for the club love to play ball. They'd rather do that than work, and anytime a player asks them to practice with him they jump at the chance. "Sure," he said. "Wait a second, I'll get you some stuff to wear."

He gave me a pair of road-gray pants, a sweat shirt, and white sanitaries. While I changed he went to get some balls and to tell the ground crew to put up the batting cage. My heart began to race. I was getting that edgy feeling I always get before a ball-game. We have a little room at one end of the clubhouse where we all keep our spare bats. I went in there and picked out a couple of my favorite models. Then I grabbed a helmet with an ear flap on the left side and went out to meet Moe.

When I got on the field it was eerie. I hadn't seen Fenway Park very often when there was no one there, and except for the people cleaning up in the stands the place was empty. Moe tossed me a ball and we started playing catch along the base line, just to get our arms loose. Finally I said, "Okay, let's go. I'm ready." Moe went to the mound and I headed toward home plate.

As I stepped into the batter's box I suddenly realized this was the spot where I'd been hit. It gave me a cold feeling. I wondered if I really could make it back all the way and I remember telling myself that if I ever did I wasn't going to be gun-shy. I'll dig in and crowd the plate like I always did, I told myself. That was my way and I wasn't going to change it. I wasn't going to let it bother me. Then I told myself, "I can think about it all I want—it isn't going to change anything."

"Okay, Moe," I yelled out. "I'll lay a couple of bunts down first." He nodded and tossed one in. I got the thick part of my bat on it and dropped it down the line. It was a good bunt. I tried several more, mostly to get the feel again, and when I finally felt ready I called out, "Okay, I'm hitting. Just throw strikes."

Moe nodded again, went into a big windmill windup, kicked his leg up and threw me a powderpuff. He weighed all of 120 pounds and he really couldn't throw the ball very hard. I hit the ball weakly to short. I hadn't seen the ball very well and I didn't get all of my bat on it. But I didn't really care at this point; all I wanted to do was hit the baseball. Anyway I could. I didn't care how far I hit it or how well; I just wanted to get the sensation of hitting a baseball again. I have always loved hitting. When I was a kid I used to hit till my hands bled. Now I just wanted to prove to myself that I could come back, no matter how long it took. I couldn't stand the thought of being away from baseball.

Moe threw me another one like the first one and I topped it down the third-base line. I missed the next one completely. It was a high inside pitch, a pitch I'd normally lay off of. Before my injury if I had decided to go for it I would have got wood on it. But not now.

I could see Moe was concerned. I realized he was worried about coming too close and maybe hitting me. The year before, when my old buddy Tony Horton was with the club he was out with an injury for a while and would come down on off-days to work out. He had Moe pitch to him. One day Moe came too close and hit him and the kid was shook up about it. Now he was afraid of hitting me.

"Look," I called out. "Don't worry about hitting me. I'm wearing a helmet and it's got an ear flap on it, and if you happen to come close I'll be able to get out of the way. Okay?"

He nodded. He's only about seventeen or eighteen, a freshman in college at the University of Massachusetts at Amherst and a serious kid by nature. His father is a dentist in Chelsea and I think Moe is studying dentistry at school. Now he got serious and began aiming the ball right down the middle. He got a good one over but the best I could do with it was send a fly ball to shallow center field. I swung and missed at a couple more and I could feel the hairs on the back of my neck pinch. I wasn't mad at Moe and I really wasn't mad at myself. I don't know exactly who I was mad at, but I was good and mad. I realized I could see the ball only with my right eye. When I tried to get the ball in my left eye, I'd lose it; the eye would tear and I'd see even less of it.

"Come on, Moe," I said, pounding the plate with my bat. "Just throw strikes!"

"I'm trying my hardest," he said. "Just remember I'm an infielder, not a pitcher."

That broke me up, but I don't think I showed it. "Okay, I'll remember that," I told him. "Let's go."

37

I hit a lot more weak ground balls, when I hit anything. Here was this little 120-pound kid throwing and all I could do was to tap grounders. I had hit 104 home runs in my four years with the Red Sox and now I could barely hit one out to shortstop. "Was that a strike?" I called out when I let one go by on the outside. "No," he said. "Low and away." I really couldn't tell. Dr. Regan was right. I couldn't judge anything. I was swinging at anything that I thought was in the strike zone, but I really couldn't tell. That's how bad it was. I swung and missed at maybe a dozen balls all day. But I wasn't embarrassed. I realized I was trying to start all over again. I knew I was hitting with only one eye.

I stayed in the cage for almost an hour. I felt sorry for poor little Moe. He must have thrown me a couple of hundred pitches, but nothing seemed to work. I'd close my left eye and try hitting with my right eye. I concentrated extra hard, really staring the ball in, and then I'd pop one up. It was more than simply my timing being off. I'd been out with injuries several times in the past or I'd lay off because I had to fulfill Army Reserve duty. I'd come to the park and have someone throw to me. My reflexes weren't as sharp after a layoff, but I could always get good wood on the ball and pump a couple on the screen. This was different. I wasn't seeing the ball. And you can't hit when you can't see.

"That's it for today, Moe," I finally told him.

He let his breath out. He was sweating, and I could see how tired he was. "Boy," he said, laughing, "I'd better put my arm in the washing machine now." I smiled too. That was a big joke around the clubhouse. Usually when a ballplayer has a sore or tired arm he puts it in the whirlpool. But Moe was so little we used to tell him all he'd need to use was the washing machine. I went inside, took a shower and got a rub from Vinnie Orlando,

38

who does the same thing for Mr. Yawkey every day. "How'd it go out there, Tony?" he asked me.

"Don't ask, Vinnie," I told him. "It'll make you sick."

A week later I had my next appointment at Dr. Regan's office. They ran me through the same tests again and found no change. My vision was still 20/100 and my distance judgment was still poor. After his people were through with me Dr. Regan sat me down in his office to tell me just how things were. "The blind spot is still there, Tony," he said. "It hasn't improved since last week, but then it hasn't gotten any worse either. You still have a good deal of swelling in there and your distance vision is so poor that it might be dangerous for you to play any more ball this year."

There it was. Somebody finally had said it to me. Now I had the word. "There's no way," Dr. Regan said, "you could get ready in time to play in the World Series if the Red Sox make it." We set up another appointment for October and I left. The next day the Red Sox announced that I was through for the year.

I had to be alone and I went back to my apartment. It's only a short walk from Fenway Park. After the games I used to find kids hanging around the hallway waiting for me. Somehow, they found out I lived there. But there was nobody around now. It was almost like they knew I wanted to be left alone. I lived on the tenth floor of a modern building. My apartment overlooked the ballpark. I stood by myself on the balcony for most of the afternoon trying to fight down the things going through my mind. I began to cry. Later on, when the game started, I stood out there in the dark and watched Ken Harrelson playing my position. I could hear the crowd howling and I realized how nice the ballpark looked with all those lights on. I realized how much I missed it now and I wished I were there playing again. I knew I belonged

39

there and could help the club and yet I wasn't there and I had strong doubts about ever playing again.

For the first time I realized how much I loved it all, how I missed the guys and the excitement of being with them and all the laughs we had. I missed the games, the competition, especially now with the ballclub fighting for the pennant. There wasn't anything in the world I would rather have been doing than playing baseball. I didn't want to go out with the best-looking girl in the world or with this actress or that model. I didn't want to own my own nightclub. I didn't want anything but to play baseball again. You don't know how much you miss something until it's taken away from you. A lot of times when I was playing I'd get to the point where I'd say, "Ah, I gotta go to the ballpark again today." I'd gripe because the season was too long. I realized what a complainer I had become, grousing about too much travel, too much this, too much that. But, boy, when it's taken away from you you'd take all those things that go with baseball and love every minute of it. These are the things I thought about standing out there on that balcony watching Ken Harrelson playing my position. The tears came and I couldn't do anything to stop them. It got so bad the following season when I was out of baseball altogether that I finally had to ask the building manager to give me an apartment that faced the other way.

Even though I wasn't going to play for the rest of the season I continued to go back to the ballpark when the team was away. I'd never hit when they were home. But I just had to keep trying, doctors or no doctors. It was about the same every time. Moe would throw up those bloopers of his and I'd tap one in the infield. Sometimes, I got so disgusted I'd call it quits early and run in the outfield instead, telling myself I was keeping my legs in shape. But my mind was racing with all kinds of doubts. Would

I ever be able to see well enough with my left eye to hit the way I used to? The last time I went out, just before the World Series, I hit a couple of balls on top of the screen. I can't tell you what it felt like even if they were hit off the mush Moe was throwing. It gave me the feeling I wasn't dead yet.

The season was down to the last few days. When the club got home I went to the ballpark every day. But of course I wouldn't go near the cage. I'd suit up and shag fly balls in the outfield, still fielding them on hops. I was trying to convince everyone that I was just keeping in shape and staying away from the writers. Whenever they cornered me at my locker and asked me about the eye, I told them the same thing, that it was coming along fine but there was no way I'd be ready to play again that season. "I'm just looking forward to getting a good winter's rest and coming back in 1968," I told them. Even if I had anything more I wanted to say, I wouldn't have told them. A few of the Boston writers and I have had feuds over the years and I wasn't interested in giving them any stories they could blow up.

Then I got some great news for a change. Dick O'Connell, our general manager, told me I'd be able to sit on the bench for the last game of the season. He'd gotten special permission from the Commissioner's office. I wanted to be there, to be part of it. After beating the Twins the previous day on Carl Yastrzemski's three-run homer, we were now tied for first place with the Twins. The Tigers were still in it too, but they had a doubleheader with the Angels. The White Sox had been in it till the final week when they knocked themselves out by losing a doubleheader to the Athletics. So, going into the last day of the season, we had to win to be sure of at least a tie, and if the Tigers lost one of their games, we were in. That's how close it was.

That last game I sat on the bench and cheered myself hoarse.

I screamed so loud that I lost my voice completely. I took a seat in the corner of the dugout right near the bat rack, and as each guy came by to go up to the plate I said something to him. George Scott was using one of my bats those days and I remember saying, "Come on, Scotty, rip one." Still, it was a strange feeling, being there in the dugout in uniform and not being able to play.

The Twins took a 2–0 lead and it stayed that way for five innings. Meanwhile, we could see on the scoreboard that the Tigers were leading in the first game against the Angels. The crowd screamed on every pitch, especially when we scored 5 runs in the sixth inning. Now I knew we'd do it. Jim Lonborg, who'd already won 21 games for us, was pitching. He'd had a great year and was a tough competitor, and I knew he wasn't going to let the Twins have the game now. They got to him for another run but he still looked plenty strong.

Out in Detroit the Tigers won their opener, but they fell behind early in the second game. I almost couldn't breathe. If the Tigers lost that game and we won this one, we were in—American League champions. The Twins threatened in the ninth inning, but Lonny hung on and got the last out. We won the game, 5–3, and after the last out it looked like everybody in the city of Boston jumped onto the field and began mobbing the players. I could see Lonny being lifted by the fans as he tried to get away and I ducked down the runway and headed up the stairs to the clubhouse.

The place was already packed with writers and TV guys and a lot of other people. But nobody did any celebrating yet. The game in Detroit was still going on. We had the radio turned on and everybody who was close enough to hear it would pass the word back almost pitch by pitch. The Angels were leading, 8–3, after the fifth inning. Jim McGlothlin was pitching for the Angels and somebody yelled out, "Come on, Mac. Hold 'em. Pour it in there." We must have stood around on pins and needles for nearly two hours, but then Dick McAuliffe of the Tigers hit into a double play that ended the game.

Suddenly, there was champagne and screaming in the packed clubhouse. We had been a 100–1 shot this year and we'd taken the pennant: The Impossible Dream. The guys were pounding each other on the back; the noise was so deafening I couldn't hear myself screaming. It was wild. But all of a sudden a terrible feeling of depression came over me. What was I feeling so good about? The feeling hit me that maybe I'd never be able to make it back again and even though I tried to throw it out of my mind it kept coming back to me. The eye was no good. It wasn't coming around. Would it ever come around? I kept trying to push it out of my mind, telling myself, *I gotta do it, I gotta do it. I can do it.* I was sitting in front of my locker and I broke into tears. I couldn't stop myself. Mike Ryan was cheering next to me and when he saw me crying he put his arm around me. "What's wrong, roomie?" he said. I shook him off. "It's nothing," I told him. "Just what the hell did I do? What did I contribute?"

"You helped," Mike said. "Sure you did. You know that. Come on, that's nothing to cry about. Damn it, we're champs!"

But I was so choked up I could hardly answer him. I just kept shaking my head and letting the tears roll down my face and telling myself that I wasn't really part of it.

"No, no, Mike," I said finally. "I'm not part of it. And now I won't be able to play in the Series either. What am I doing here anyway? I don't belong here. This is your party, you guys won it."

Then Tom Yawkey was at my side. He put his two arms around me and hugged me and said, "Tony, you helped. You were a part of it. Those games you won for us in the early part of the season,

43

well, they're just as important as today's game. You helped. You contributed." But I just kept shaking my head back and forth. "Hold your head up high, Tony," Mr. Yawkey said. "Without you we don't win the pennant."

"Come on roomie, you're gonna make me cry," Mike said.

Rico was there too. "Hey," he said. "Remember that homer you hit in Chicago? What about that, and all the others you hit for us this year? You hit 20 homers this year. Don't you know you helped us win it? Come on, kid."

I made a pretense that everything was okay, but I got away from the celebration as soon as I could. The following day I got word that the Commissioner's office was letting me dress and sit on the bench during the World Series.

The St. Louis Cardinals had won the pennant in the National League. We knew they were loaded with guys like Bob Gibson, Lou Brock, Orlando Cepeda, Curt Flood, Roger Maris, and Tim McCarver. Frank Malzone, who used to play third base for the Red Sox, scouted the Cards the last few weeks of the season and brought back a tremendous report on them. Williams went over their lineup from top to bottom with us. We knew them so well we practically knew how many times each guy went to the bathroom during a game. That's how thoroughly Malzone had scouted them.

Since Lonborg had pitched the clincher, Williams decided to open the Series with Jose Santiago. Jose had been a big man down the stretch for us, winning his last eight starts. He's one of the nicest guys I've ever played with and he and I had become pretty close during the season. If you don't know him he looks like a pretty serious guy, but he also has his funny side. Jose thinks he's Dracula and likes to go around the clubhouse saying things like "Tony, my darling. Let me bite you in the neck."—with an accent and all—"I vant to dreenk your blood." That always cracks us up. But when I sat down to talk to him before his Series start he wasn't Dracula. He was dead serious.

"Boy, you had a great year and I know your gonna beat those guys today," I told him. "I just know it." Jose just nodded. "I hope so, Tony," he said. "We win the first one, we're on our way. That's the important one."

I stopped at Ellie Howard's locker and told him what a great job he had done with our pitching staff since he joined us. He'd been through this kind of thing plenty of times before with the Yankees, but I could see he was just as tense as the rest of the guys. I went around the clubhouse and tried to say something cheerful to each of the guys before the game. What else was there for me to do? I figured a couple of words would help loosen them up. I stopped at Yaz's locker and knew the pressure that was on his shoulders today. He looked cool and ready; but he never seems up tight, even when he is.

I juiced Rico pretty good before he went out to the field. "Is your brother here today, Rico?" I said innocently. "Yeah," he said, pretending to be sad. Every time Rico's brother shows up at a game Rico doesn't hit. At least that's the way it seems to us and we're always telling Rico to keep him away from the ballpark. "You should have sent him to Hawaii," I told him. Rico laughed, rapped me in the belly with his glove, and went out.

I saved the Boomer for last. That's George Scott. He's always hanging around me, and he's truly one of the funniest people I know. I've never seen a guy maintain his confidence like the Boomer, even when he's in the worst kind of slump. I've also never met anybody who's more superstitious. He'll spend half an hour before a game examining each one of his bats, looking for the ones with hits in them. He talks to them. He'll grip a bat and say, "You got any hits in you today?" Then he'll pump it a few times with those powerful wrists of his and throw it down on the floor and say, "You ain't got nothin'!" Then he'll pick up another one and do the same thing until it's time to go out. By then he's sure he's found the right bats. And when he has a good one he'll lock it up in our little bat room so that nobody else will find it.

"How you feeling today, Boomer?" I asked him.

"Hey, T.C., T.C.," he said. "Somebody's gonna get hurt out there today."

"What are you talking about, George?" I said.

"I'm gonna hang out some peas today and anybody gets in the way is gonna get hurt," he answered with the most serious expression on his face.

Then he starts saying, "I can do it, I can do it, I can do it." And then he goes to the mirror and looks into it and says, "You can do it, George."

When I look back on it now I don't know how much good I did. Everybody was so preoccupied thinking they were playing in a World Series that I don't think they heard a word I said anyway. They were all so keyed up, I think a few guys were surprised to see me in uniform. They weren't paying much attention to me, but I figured I had to try anyway.

That's another thing about being in the Series. It heals all wounds, or at least makes them unimportant. I forgot all about being sore at Dick Williams and I'm sure he didn't give me a thought. I couldn't blame him for that. He was a rookie manager who'd won a pennant and he had to think about beating the Cardinals. Anything between him and me was forgotten during the Series.

During pregame practice I didn't work out at all. But I wanted to feel a part of things so I wandered around a lot. When the

Cardinals took infield practice I happened to be standing near first base and Orlando Cepeda looked over at me. "Hey Tony," he said. "How's the eye?" I made a circle with the fingers on my right hand and nodded at him. "That a boy," he said. "Stay with 'em, big guy. Stay with 'em. You'll be back." It felt great to hear him say that. I thought to myself, here's a guy on the other team taking the time to think about me.

Just before the start of the game I got the shock of my life. They began to introduce the players of both teams, first the Cardinals, then the Red Sox. As each player had his name called out he ran out of the dugout and stood on the base line. I was sitting in the dugout, half listening to the names when I heard the voice over the P.A. system say, "And now, one of the major contributors to the Red Sox victory . . . a player who because of injury is not eligible to play, but due to special permission of the Commissioner of Baseball will be sitting on the Red Sox bench . . . number 25, Tony Conigliaro." I was frozen. All of a sudden the crowd was standing up cheering, and I found myself trotting out on the field. Don't ask me who was standing next to me; I was too numb to know what was going on. I stood there and they seemed to be cheering me all the way back to Swampscott. I felt the tears coming and there was no use trying to hold them back. It was beautiful.

I always knew Bob Gibson was a great pitcher. I had hit against him in exhibition games in Florida, but he really showed me how great he was in the Series. In the first game he just blew the ball by our hitters. He beat us, 2–1, striking out 10 and walking only 1. He almost made it look easy. Poor Jose, he didn't have it this day. He pitched on his guts mostly and hung in there for seven innings. The Cards had him in trouble nearly every inning, but the best they could do was get single runs off him in the third

and seventh. It was Brock who hurt him both times. He led off
with a hit each time, stole a base once and scored both runs. We
got our run in the third when Jose ripped a two-strike pitch and
hit it on the screen for a homer. It was the only bad pitch Gibson
made all day.

The next day Lonborg made it almost impossible for the Cards
to beat us again. He wound up throwing a one-hitter and we won,
5–0. For a while Lonny was working on a perfect game. Then in
the seventh he walked Curt Flood to give the Cards their first
base runner. The no-hitter lasted another inning, until Julian
Javier doubled with two down in the eighth. It's too bad Lonny had
to lose the no-hitter. He pitched his heart out. He'd come back to
the dugout after each inning, little drops of sweat dripping down
his face. But he was expressionless. He didn't talk to anybody;
he'd slip on his warm-up jacket and sit down. Sometimes he
paced. I felt like pacing with him, but I knew I'd better keep my
distance. Besides I was busy trying to keep the hitters alive. Not
that they needed my help. The guys pounded the Cards' pitching
for 9 hits and Yaz smacked 2 homers. Now it was all even and
we felt good about winning one in front of our own fans. Then
it was off to St. Louis where the Series would be played for the
next three games.

Before we left for St. Louis I ran into Sandy Koufax. He had
just retired from baseball because of an arthritic condition in his
pitching arm and was covering the Series for NBC. He asked me
if I was going to St. Louis with the ballclub. "I sure am," I told
him.

"Fine," he said. "I'd like to have you on my pregame show
before the third game on Saturday. We tape it in advance. Will
you come on with me?" I told him sure and he said he'd call me
at my hotel the morning of the game.

He phoned me early Saturday morning and we met at the local TV station in St. Louis. When the cameras began to roll Sandy introduced me and explained how I happened to get hit in the head and had to miss playing in the Series. Then he turned to me and asked how I thought the Series would turn out, and I told him the Red Sox were going to win it because I really thought so. Then he turned to me seriously and said it was too bad I had to get hit that way and miss out on the Series, and he asked me the condition of my eye. "It's far from 100 percent," I told him. "There isn't anything in the world I'd rather be doing than playing in this World Series, but the eye just isn't improved enough to let me back now." But I told him I was sure it would be okay for the 1968 season and I tried to sound convincing. The whole thing ran about ten minutes and when it was over Sandy invited me to have lunch with him.

Over lunch I said, "Do you miss baseball, Sandy, now that you're out of it? Are you sorry you're not playing anymore?"

"Tony," he said, "you never realize how much you love the game until you're not playing it anymore. Sure I miss it a lot."

"Would you like to be back in it right now if you could?" I asked.

He didn't answer for a couple of seconds and I thought maybe I had asked the wrong question. "It was probably for the best that I quit when I did," Sandy finally said. He told me how much the arm had bothered him and the risk he'd have run if he had continued to play baseball. I think I knew how he felt.

Then we got on the subject of marriage. "How come you've managed to stay single all these years?" I asked him. (Of course, he got married a year later, but at this time he was still one of the most eligible bachelors around.) Sandy laughed. "I don't know," he said. "I guess I still don't think I'm ready for marriage."

49

Then I told him my half of the story. "I can't imagine living with one person for the rest of my life," I said, "and I wouldn't know how to make the decision if I had to. I let too many things bother me and I want to be free. I'd be a tough guy to live with."

"Don't worry about it," Sandy told me. "Stay free and when the time comes you'll know it." The waitress came with the check and when I grabbed for it I thought Sandy would bite my head off. "This lunch is on me," he said. "You owe me one in Boston." After that we walked to the ballpark together.

The Cards beat us in the third game, 5–2. It was one of those games that started right for them and followed its course. Lou Brock tripled in the first inning and came home on Curt Flood's single. Gary Bell started for us and he lasted only two innings. By then the score was 3–0. Sometime during the game I looked out toward the scoreboard and realized that I couldn't make out the numbers. I'd look at them and they'd be all jumbled up. I closed my right eye and it was worse than having them both open; I couldn't make out a single number with my left eye. I did this every day after that to see if there was any change, but it was always the same. I began to feel more and more discouraged; I didn't have much to yell about that day.

At night I went out for dinner with some of the guys. They made it obvious they wanted me around and it made me feel good, but to tell the truth I wasn't good company. I really preferred being by myself and I was glad that Rico and some of my other close friends on the club brought their wives with them to St. Louis. This made it easier for me to be alone, and I even roomed by myself. But the guys kept on trying. They always wanted to know where I was going after the game, what I was going to do. We were still like a very close family. Nothing had changed for them, but I wasn't playing and that made a big difference to me. When I look back on those three days it was a very quiet time.

We lost again the next day and now the Cards were one game away from taking the Series. Santiago and Gibson were pitching and once again we were out of the game early. They scored four big runs in the first inning, and you can't give Gibson that kind of edge. The final score was 6–0. When you can't put any runs on the board what's the difference what the score is, 1–0 or 6–0? They're all the same. I looked around the clubhouse after the game, and the guys were hanging their heads. We had a great hitting team and it hurt them that they weren't scoring. Yaz more than anybody. But that's the way he is; he enjoys and suffers more than any ballplayer I've ever known. He can get a team up just by the way he behaves before a game, slapping guys on the back, saying, "Come on, we can do it." Then, of course, he goes out and does most of it himself. When he's down it isn't for long. Mostly, he's down on himself for not doing more, even when he's done more than his own share.

Lonborg was going for us the next day in the do-or-die game. Lonny was phenomenal, just the way he'd been all year. That 1967 season he was one hell of a competitor. You'd see him walk out to the mound and knew he was going to win; it was a pleasure to be playing behind him. He'd stand glaring at the hitters, just daring them to take a good toehold, then he'd throw that ball right down their throats. Nothing frightened him. The Cards could hardly touch him. They got 3 hits, and we won the game, 3–1. They didn't get their run till the ninth inning. The impressive thing is the way he protected a 1–0 lead into the eighth. That's how tough he was.

In the ninth Ellie Howard singled with the bases loaded. One run scored on the hit and another when Roger Maris' throw to the plate was high. I was leaping up and down in the dugout. I looked out at Ellie standing on first base and he looked like the biggest man in the world. He'd been a great asset to the club ever since we got him from the Yankees. From the first day he joined our ballclub, I don't think I ever saw one of our pitchers ever shake off one of his signs. Usually a pitcher will stare down from the mound and if he doesn't like what he sees he shakes his head and waits till the catcher comes up with something he wants. But not with Ellie. They had too much respect for him. He gave them confidence, and I know after the Series Lonborg paid tribute to Ellie when he said that having him behind the plate took the burden of thinking off his own shoulders. The win meant we'd be going back to Boston to play in front of our own fans again.

In the sixth game we finally played our kind of game and won. Our kind of game is a slugging game, and our hitters came through to tie the Series up. Gary Waslewski, a young pitcher who sometimes looked like Lonborg, was our starter. He was an untried rookie and we were going with him because he had pitched three great innings of relief in the third game. In the second inning Rico hit one on the screen to give us a 1–0 lead. When he got back to the dugout I was the first guy to grab him and and wrap him in my arms. "We're far from finished," I screamed. "We're coming back, we're coming back." But the game turned out to be a seesaw battle. The Cards scored 2 runs in the third and we came back with 3 in the fourth. Yaz led off the inning by hitting one up on the screen. That tied the score at 2–2. After Harrelson and Scotty had made outs, Smith came up and homered down the line in right. Next Rico hit his second homer of the game. Our dugout really exploded when we saw Rico's shot go out; you would have thought we had just won the entire Series. The Cards came back in the next inning to tie the game up again, but we won it in the bottom of the seventh by scoring 4 runs. We were back even with the Cards; it was a great comeback. I hadn't played a single inning and yet I felt exhausted.

Boston was a great place to be then. I think everybody in the city was in love with the Red Sox and with each other. Boston has always been a fine baseball town, win or lose; but it's always a lot better when you're winners. Cab drivers were happy, the traffic at Kenmore Square near the ballpark was at a standstill, but nobody seemed to care. People stood on top of their cars and cheered. Nobody was in a rush or cared about anything but the Red Sox.

It's lucky we had only one more game to play. We had run out of pitchers. Williams started Lonborg on two days' rest. You couldn't blame him—there was nobody else and I know Lonny wanted to pitch. Gibson was going for the Cardinals, with one more day of rest than Lonny. When Lonny came into the club-house I had never seen him look so bad. He was very pale; his cheeks were sunken; he looked completely exhausted, drained. I felt sorry for him.

I went over and sat down by him and asked him how he felt. He said he was fine. "We gotta do it today," I told him. "This is it, the whole thing." He looked up from his chair. "I know it," he said, "and I'm gonna do it. Don't worry. I'll do it." But I had a feeling he was really hoping that his arm would hold out. He was tired and there was no way of hiding it. I hated to see him have to walk out to the mound.

The Cards didn't score till the third. Dal Maxvill, a weak hitter, tripled to deep center field. "Oh, no," I said to myself. When a guy like him hits a ball that far it's a mistake. I felt Jim didn't have much on the ball, but he got the next two guys somehow. Then Flood singled for the run. Maris singled after him and they

53

had first and third with 2 out. Then Lonny let go a wild pitch and they had their second run. If Gibson was tired he didn't show it. He set us down in order during the first four innings. The Cards continued to tag Jim and scored a couple of more runs in the fifth. Now it was 4–0. Scotty led off for us in the fifth, using one of my bats, and tripled for our first hit. He scored on a wild peg, but that's all we got that inning.

I think we knew the end was in sight when Julian Javier hit a 3-run homer in the sixth. When that ball left Javier's bat, I could feel the tremendous letdown on our bench. Something went out of us and I felt sick. Gibson looked to me like he was tiring late in the game, but you could see him reach back for that little bit extra and he finished strong.

The final score was 7–2. As soon as Scotty fanned for the final out we filed off the bench and headed for the locker room. It was like a funeral march. Everybody went immediately to his locker and sat with his head down. For a moment I stood in the middle of the room, proud of these guys. They had battled their way to a pennant against 100–1 odds, winning it on the last day of the season in a four-team race, then came back in the Series after being down three games to one. There was nothing to be ashamed of, everything to be proud of. I actually had to fight back tears.

Mike Andrews, who had a great rookie year at second base for us, was in a corner of the room and the tears were pouring down his face in buckets. Yaz went around from one guy to the next slapping them on the ass telling them what a great job they had done. Soon the guys began talking quietly to each other and to the writers who came in to see our wake. Everybody realized it was finally all over. We had been beaten by a hell of a ballclub.

I don't think anybody on the ballclub will ever forget the experience we had of playing together that season. I never thought such closeness between men was possible. I'd never seen anything like it before. Lots of guys were crying. Lonborg looked like he was in a daze and was going around apologizing to everybody; tears were in his eyes. Scotty and Rico hugged one another in silence. Ellie Howard stopped by my locker and looked like he had just lost his best friend. He'd played in nine World Series during his great years with the Yankees and this should have been old hat to him, but he said to me, "Tony, this one meant as much to me as any one of the others I've been in."

I was both happy and sorry the season was over. I was happy because now I didn't have to eat my heart out that I wasn't playing. But I was sad because now there was nothing to keep my mind off my eye. Since my last exam I hadn't noticed any change. The numbers on the scoreboard were as fuzzy in the seventh game as they were in the first. I was still tipping over glasses at home unless I was very careful. I would constantly close my right eye to see if the distortion area was getting smaller, but it was the same. When I drove my car at night headlights were blurry.

When I went back for my next appointment at the Retina Associates I was put through the same tests as before. Now I realized that they were taking these to compare with the previous tests. I can't say I ever enjoyed it and I never looked forward to going there. Molly McCormick was always telling me how jumpy I was. I felt these people knew what they were doing and that they could really tell me about the condition of my eye. But the only thing I wanted to hear them tell me was that I'd play ball again. I wasn't interested in hearing anything else. Taking the same tests over and over again really got to me and I gave them a hard time.

When they were through with me this time Dr. Regan sat me down as usual and told me things had quieted down inside the eye. My vision had improved to 20/50, mostly because the swelling had gone down a lot in the six weeks since my last visit. But he warned me about getting optimistic too soon. He explained that although I was seeing things with less distortion, the balance was poor between the two eyes. He told me the blind spot had nearly disappeared, except for what was left of the small cyst; he said he didn't know how much more improvement there would be.

"You mean I'm going to stay at 20/50?" I asked him.

"Possibly," he answered. "It's problematical at this time."

"Does this mean I can't play ball anymore?" I was beginning to panic.

"No, I wouldn't say that either," he said. One thing about doctors, I found out they never commit themselves. This uncertainty exasperated me. "If the defect in one eye is small," he explained, "then it can be compensated for by the right eye when both of them are open. Right now, there is a big imbalance between the vision in your right eye and the vision in your left eye. But when both your eyes are open, what we call binocular vision, it's possible to get a balance."

"Then what do I do?" I asked him. "You're not really telling me anything."

"I think it's something you'll have to find out for yourself," Dr. Regan said. "We can't predict how it will be for you because there's no way of knowing. It's an individual thing. Playing baseball is performing a skilled task. Under these circumstances, one individual may be able to do it while another may not."

I was still stuck with no answers. Dr. Regan wanted me to come back again next month and I nearly said, "What the hell for? We're not making any progress. All we're doing is having my eye poked and picked at and then finding out it's still far from normal."

When I look back on those days I don't know how I didn't go

crazy. All my life things had just happened. I had been lucky the way everything just seemed to go my way all the time. I never thought about tomorrow. I never had any doubts that tomorrow would come and turn out all right. Now for the first time in my life, I just didn't know what tomorrow would bring. And nobody else did either. I was sick and confused inside, and the worst part of it was that I couldn't tell anybody about it. I have always kept a lot of my feelings locked up inside myself. I was close to my parents and talked to them a lot. But even with them I could only go so far. I've told myself for years that I didn't want to worry them too much, that was why I held back. But I really don't know for sure if that was the reason.

Sometime during the World Series, Joe Reichler of the Commissioner's office asked me if I'd like to visit the soldiers in Vietnam. I had mixed feelings about going. I didn't know what good I would do over there. But I also knew I wasn't doing myself any good moping around the apartment, and I really was honored that they had thought of asking me. I told him I'd be glad to go. I found out that Joe DiMaggio, Pete Rose, Jerry Coleman, and Bob Fishel of the Yankees' front office were also going. We were flown out to San Francisco where we had dinner at Joe's restaurant, and spent the first night.

We were in Vietnam for two weeks. Landing at Saigon, I found out there's no such thing as a gradual descent there because of possible ground fire; the big jets just come straight in. Saigon was supposed to be our base, but we actually spent only two nights there; the rest of the time we slept in tents somewhere in the battle zones, though I don't think we were ever exposed to much danger. I was really amazed at how interested in baseball these guys were. That's all they wanted to talk about. One of the first soldiers I met said to me, "I lost $10 on the World Series."

"I lost three grand," I answered, and he really broke up.

They broke us into two groups. DiMaggio and Rose and Fishel were sent to the south and Coleman and I were sent to the north, so that more troops could see us this way. We visited about ten hospitals, and everywhere I went, the soldiers—they were kids, really, twenty, twenty-one years old—asked me how my eye was. They all knew what had happened and it moved me to see these guys so concerned about me. But at one hospital at An Khe a young doctor came up to me and said, "Hi, Tony, how's your arm?"

I looked at him puzzled and said, "My arm's okay. It's my eye that's been injured."

"I know all about your eye," he said. "I really am talking about your arm. I treated you at Sancta Maria Hospital one day in 1966 when you got hit on the arm by a pitch."

It came back to me. This was Dr. Bob Provost and he had treated me because Dr. Tierney had been out of town that day. He heard I was coming over and had waited to see me. During my fifteen days over there I met countless guys from the Boston area and I promised them that when I got home I'd contact their families and let them know they were all right.

We saw some of the fighting but thank God it never got very close to us. Jerry and I were flown from base to base and we had two guys with machine guns assigned to us all the time. Mostly we talked baseball and we showed a film about the 1967 season. We toured hospitals, enlisted men's clubs, the Naval Club and saw thousands of kids who were fighting the war. The worst part of the trip was going into the hospitals and seeing guys all shot up. It wouldn't have been so bad if we hadn't gone through the intensive care ward, but the doctors thought it would help so we went in there. Here we found guys fresh off the battlefield. Just as we got there one day a helicopter was coming in carrying about thirteen or fourteen dead bodies and I saw them take them off like sacks of potatoes.

I met one soldier sitting in a wheel chair; he looked in awful shape. I asked the doctor how he was going to be. He said it was very hard to say, they had only operated on him the day before. He had a scar running from the bottom of his neck down to his belly button. A good portion of his skull had been ripped off. There were burn marks all over his hands and arms. The doctor asked me to walk over to him. The guy looked up at me and very slowly said, "You don't know what it means to us to have you guys come over here and see us like this. Glad to have you here." We talked for about ten minutes. Just as I started to walk away he said, "Tony, come here." I went over, and as I bent over he said to me, "How's your eye?"

Maybe for the first time I really saw how pitiful I was feeling so sorry for myself. I had only an eye injury from a baseball game, and even if I never played again what did that add up to compared to these kids who were losing their lives and coming home with broken bodies. I realized that even if I didn't get my sight back I was still a lucky guy to be alive.

After two weeks I couldn't wait to get home. It had been a long, long fifteen days, but it had given me plenty of time to think. I didn't really get away from my troubles. But I understood them better. Sure, I still wanted to see well again and play ball. I knew I'd never be happy if I couldn't. But I know I came back with a better understanding of things and for the first time really looked forward to my next eye examination. I went home with a new hope.

There's one thing I'd like to add. It's about a guy named Freddie Atkinson, the best friend I've ever had. We ran around a lot together back in Lynn when we both went to high school. I don't know what there was about Freddie, but we just hit it off together. I know I always had more money than he did, but Freddie always insisted on paying his own way.

There was the day Freddie told me he was going to Vietnam. This was 1964, when I was breaking in with the Red Sox. I felt terrible about it, and the night before he was supposed to leave we really went out and had a good time. The next day when we shook hands there seemed to be something final about the handshake. After Freddie left I went into the bathroom crying.

I guess he was in Vietnam about four months. I had just got home from a road trip and was with my mother in our new home in Swampscott. I remember she said to me, "I have something to tell you. Try not to take this too hard." Well, the first thing I thought of was maybe my grandfather was sick or that my grandmother had died. Then all she said was, "Freddie," and I knew what was coming next. I fell down on the floor and began crying. It hurt so much I was gasping for air and I thought I was going to have a heart attack.

Whenever I could, I'd go over to his house. Freddie's mother had died of cancer the year before he did, but he had a stepmother now and I'd try to cheer her and his father up. I didn't enjoy going over there because it was so eerie, but I felt he wanted me to do it. The last time I went over there, I heard what I thought was a voice. It said, "Thank you," and I believe it was Freddie's voice. He was telling me he was grateful.

It was late November when I saw Dr. Regan again. I didn't know what to expect this time. I wasn't up and I wasn't down. I had gone through this so many times it almost began to feel meaningless. I went through it almost as if it was happening to somebody else. This time there was an important change. After studying the reports from the other doctors and specialists who tested me and then examining me himself, Dr. Regan said that the inner wall of the cyst on my macula had broken. Before I could get all shook up by the way it sounded, Dr. Regan quickly said that this didn't mean the eye had grown worse; in fact, he said he could see no further deterioration and that the eye seemed to have stabilized. My vision was still 20/50, but he said the fact that the outer wall of the cyst was holding was a sign things were no worse than the last time.

Then he said he could see no reason why I couldn't resume normal physical activity. This was the first time I had ever heard those words from him. "But you'll still have to find out for yourself if you can play baseball again," Dr. Regan said. "Your eye is still not normal. It's just stabilized and it doesn't look as if it will get any worse. I'm not even sure whether you'll have more difficulty hitting a ball or catching it. Play pepper, have a catch. See how it goes. Only *you* will be able to tell when you try it."

"Well, I'm gonna try it, doc," I said. "I'm gonna do it."

It was a hopeful sign, but that was all. I didn't give a damn what the tests showed. I knew I still couldn't see. I knew things would stay up in the air until I went to spring training and swung at a live pitcher again. That's the only way I'd know for sure, the tests be damned. I knew this the minute I left Dr. Regan's office and went into the street. There was never a time I wasn't afraid of closing my right eye to see what the left eye picked up. When I looked straight out of the left eye alone, things looked fuzzy and soft, parts of things that were there I couldn't see. When I looked slightly off to one side things then looked okay. Dr. Regan had explained to me that this was my peripheral vision, and that it had not been damaged. What had been damaged was my direct vision, what they call macula vision. That's the vision that

61

lets you pick out the spin on the ball and lets you judge the distance it is from the bat you're holding in your hands. It was stabilizing; the only thing wrong with that was that I couldn't see with my left eye worth a damn.

The next few months were the most miserable period of my life. I was hard on everyone around me and on myself. I didn't go out with girls much and when I did I treated them badly if things didn't go exactly my way. I had very little patience with anyone or anything. I sulked a lot. I think the only person I even talked to was my roommate, Tony Athanas, Jr., I even mistreated my family. I love them a lot and am very close to them, but now I'd snap at my mother for nothing and wouldn't even answer a simple question from my father.

One day we were all sitting around the kitchen table in Swampscott, and my father took a baseball and said, "Look, come on, Choo, [that's a nickname he's always called me by] I have this baseball. I'll move it different distances from you and you see if you can judge how far away it is."

I slammed my fist on the table. "No, Dad," I said. "Look, I can't see. That's all. Leave me alone, will ya." Then I stormed out of the house and drove back to my apartment. I sometimes just sat there alone all day. I brooded and I was moody all the time, snapping at people. I was glum and worried. I only told people a little of the truth. I didn't want to tell them how, deep down, I was really worried. I didn't want to burden anybody, especially my parents, so I kept most of it within me. There was nobody I could tell my trouble to. So I'd sit around the apartment and eventually fall asleep. When I woke up it was dark outside and dark inside.

I gave my brother Billy a hard time, too. He's only a couple of years younger than I and was moving up in the Red Sox organization. We had always talked about the day we'd be playing in the Boston outfield together, but now with everything so uncertain I didn't give a damn. One day he came to my apartment. I was sleeping when he rang the bell. When I got to the door I saw he had a girl outside with him. I wondered what they were doing there. Billy said they wanted to watch television and could they come in for a while. Well, I really snapped his head off, asking why the hell he couldn't go watch TV somewhere else, and he wound up saying, "Okay, if that's the way you want it we'll go," and they left. I don't think we talked to each other for about two weeks.

To help pass the time and get my mind off things I organized a small rock group and sang a few dates around Boston at a place called O'Dees, which is really in Cambridge. (I had begun singing rock a couple of years earlier and made a few records.) We had an organ, drums, lead guitar, bass guitar, a sax trumpet, and trombone and we called ourselves Tony C. and the All Night Workers. We played to capacity crowds and I was invited to appear with Merv Griffin and his TV people in a show coming to the Back Bay Theater. I thought I'd enjoy performing, but it wasn't much fun with my baseball career in doubt. When I'd get back to my apartment at night I realized my problems were still there. The singing was only a stopgap. I knew I was marking time until spring training.

In January I began going out to Harvard where they had an

indoor batting cage and I worked out about twice a week till I went to spring training. Darrell Brandon, one of our pitchers, came out most of the time and pitched to me. It wasn't as private as I would have liked because somebody or other was always wandering in. But I tried to concentrate on my hitting. I knew I wasn't making good contact with the ball. It was hard to pick out and the lights in the gym weren't that good. The people who were watching didn't know what they were watching. I'd hear them say things like, "Boy, he's back in the groove again," and, "He sure looks good." But they didn't know what they were talking about.

Buddy LeRoux, our trainer, would sometimes come down and work out, too. He caught more balls on his shins and knees than anybody I ever saw in my life. I'd needle him. "Which hospital do you go to when you leave here to get those bruises fixed up?" I'd say, but he'd just laugh at me and sweat. Outwardly I was putting on a pretty good show. The only guy that wasn't fooled was me. I knew I had to talk to somebody and I trusted Buddy a lot. So before taking my shower one day I said to him, "Buddy, see me upstairs. I got to talk to you about something." He said he'd be right up.

I stayed in the shower a long time. When I heard him come in I came out and said, "Buddy, you know I've never lied to you before and I can't keep this a secret any longer. My vision is not good."

Buddy stared at me. "What are you saying, kid?" he said.

"I'm working as hard as I can at seeing that damn thing, Buddy, but it just doesn't look the same," I told him. "At times my depth perception is way off. I don't know where the hell the ball is. I don't know if I can make it this year."

Buddy shook his head and said, "I don't ever want to hear you say that again. You'll make it. Just stay with it."

I said, "I'm gonna have to do a lot of extra things to make up for my defect. It's going to be rough in Florida."

"Just keep working," Buddy said. "Don't lose your confidence. I'm sure it'll come around. You been out a long time."

I said, "Okay, but do me a favor, Buddy, and don't say a word about this to anybody. I'm going to give it 150 percent but I really don't know."

I kept going back and working out. One day while I was in the cage, Ed Penney, my business manager, came to see me. He wasn't alone. When I looked behind him I nearly fell over. One of the guys with him was Merv Griffin. With Merv was a nice guy named Bob Murphy, who handles the talent for Griffin's show. Merv had wanted to come over and meet me because I was going to appear on the same program with him at the Back Bay Theater in Boston.

He said he was a big fan of mine and asked how everything was going with my eyesight. I told him things were coming along all right. And he said, "Keep plugging. With your determination you'll bounce back." Then he looked at the bat I was holding and asked if he could take a few swings. I said sure and I got him a sweatshirt and gave him my batting helmet with the protective flap on the side. Then I went out and pitched to him. He wasn't a bad hitter. But, then, look who was doing the pitching.

I found the more I wanted spring training to begin the more the winter dragged. Finally when February came I went south a few days early with Billy and we spent a couple of days at the Doral Country Club just loosening up and getting some sun.

65

Just before we left, I told my father, "Dad, when I get to Winter Haven I'm just going to behave like another human being. It's going to be a tough comeback, if I can make it at all. I'm not going to fool around. I'll be in bed every night at eleven o'clock. I'm going to eat steaks and take care of myself. I'm going to bear down. I'm going to work harder than any human being ever worked in baseball."

"I know you're going to do it, Choo," he said to me, and he just took me and hugged me. "Vinnie and I'll be down to see you in a couple of days. I know everything's going to be all right."

Billy and I got to Winter Haven for the first day of camp. Naturally the guys were all glad to see me, Rico and Boomer and Ellie Howard. It was like an old-fashioned reunion in the clubhouse. The guys swarmed around me and told me how good I looked and wished me luck. Dick Williams took me aside and told me I could train at my own pace. "You're on your own this spring, Tony," he said. "You can do anything you want. I won't push you. When you're ready to play in a game just let me know. If there are some pitchers who are going to give you trouble we'll just keep you out of the lineup. Everything's up to you this spring." I guessed that's all the man had to say to me. He never once asked me how my eye was, or how I felt, or said anything about not coming to see me when I was in the hospital. Okay, I said to myself, that's the way it is. But I know I let it get under my skin.

I tried to put my feelings about Williams out of my mind. But it was really very difficult. Already, I could feel the pressure building up. Two weeks into the spring I felt there must have been 100 sets of eyes watching me. My father and my Uncle Vinnie and a lot of neighbors from Swampscott were all around me now. And everytime I'd hit one I could hear one of them say,

"Wow, look at that. The kid looks good." I didn't mind having them there. I know they meant well. I know I needed my father around. But the pressure was becoming something terrific. I was facing a difficult comeback and now I had my whole family and the Boston press in addition to my teammates watching my every move. Everybody was shouting advice to me. I felt like I was under a microscope, and all I wanted was some privacy so I could work things out for myself.

I hit against the machines for the first three days, and I must have hit about 300 balls a day. I was encouraged by some of the balls I hit. After my first day in the cage, Williams walked away with a satisfied look on his face. "You're doing all right," he said. Later he told the writers, "I have a hunch that Tony is going to have that big, big year in 1968."

Finally I decided it was time to face live pitching. I think Dick Ellsworth was the first pitcher I hit against in camp. He's a big left-hander with good stuff, but of course this was early for both of us. He wasn't trying to do much more than get the ball over. I'm also sure he never intended to come anywhere near me. That was another thing I had to face at the start of my comeback. Knowing that the pitchers on my club were going to be a little timid with me. Nobody wanted to take a chance of my not being able to get out of the way of the ball. I took only five swings and lined one of the pitches over the wall in left. I had quite a crowd behind the cage watching me and everyone got very excited. But I knew it was too early to tell anything. Sure, I had made contact, but against straight pitching.

Next time I got in the cage Bill Landis, another lefty, was pitching. This time I lined one over the fence in right. It felt great watching the ball sail out of the park. I could see the ball pretty well, but not like before. It was different. I really couldn't

67

pick it out like I once did. I found I really had to concentrate extra hard to follow the ball the second it left the pitcher's hand. Sometime before it got to home plate it would start to fuzz up and I swung at it just before I lost complete sight of it.

The day before we were supposed to go to Sarasota to play the White Sox in the first exhibition game I was sitting around my locker in Winter Haven and there were about twenty writers around. One writer said to me, "Tony, what would you do if you knew now that someone was deliberately trying to throw at you to hurt you?" After all I'd been through, this question really rubbed me the wrong way, and I said, "I'll go out to that goddamned mound with a bat and I'll bang him on the head with it." I meant it at the time because the question just hit me the wrong way.

Well, all of a sudden the story was picked up by Jimmy Mann in St. Petersburg, and I'll never forgive this guy for writing what he wrote. He quoted me as saying, "If anybody ever brushes me back I'm going to go out to the mound and break my bat over his head." Now, this was awful. I never said what he wrote. I had never in my life gone after a pitcher in that way. I meant what I said, but I said I'd have to know it was deliberate. But the way Mann put it, I was challenging anybody who even brushed me back and I never said that. He never put the question in the paper the way it was asked in Winter Haven. It was just another case of a writer going after a story his way.

The fact is I never had been too careful when giving interviews to writers, but then neither have they been too careful to put things down the way they were said and not the way they like to see them said. I wasn't going after any pitchers who brushed me back or knocked me down. That's part of the game and I expect it; and I have been knocked down many times. When I caught up to Mann in Sarasota I said, "What did you write that for?" And he answered, "You said it."

"The hell I did," I told him, and then I repeated what I had said for publication. He then apologized, but I walked away from him. I'm still sore at him, even though he did write a retraction the next day. But he knew what he was doing all the time, and so do most of the other guys who write that way.

Anyway, the damage had already been done. I wanted to play in the first exhibition. I told Williams I was ready and he put me in the lineup. Tommy John was on the mound for the White Sox and he knocked me down on the first pitch. I'm sure it would have got me in the head if I hadn't gotten out of the way in time. I'll never forgive him for that. He probably read that Jimmy Mann story and didn't like being challenged. If I was a pitcher and I'd read those things I would have done the same thing. Later on in the game I got hit in the ribs by Don McMahon. This is how I spent my first day back in baseball. But the funny thing is those are the only two times pitchers tried to knock me down in spring training.

I know I wasn't afraid. When I got to spring training I had moved away from the plate about six inches from where I used to stand. I've always crowded the plate, which probably explains why I've been hit so many times in my career. But I've always felt the plate belongs to me. I've always been an aggressive hitter; I attack the ball. Later on I began inching closer to the plate. I never got back as close as before, but it was close enough. I wasn't afraid of being hit. I wasn't gun-shy. I was wearing a helmet with an ear flap on the left side that covered the area where I'd been hit, so I felt protected enough. I was never afraid of the ball.

I didn't play the next day because Williams wanted to look over some of the other players, including my brother Billy. But the following day I played against the Athletics and hit a double and single as we won, 14–4. A couple of days after that I knocked in a run with a single to help beat the White Sox. This took some of the pressure off me, because the writers stopped watching everything I was doing and I was being left alone more. But I knew the blind spot was still there because I wasn't seeing all of the ball. I was seeing enough of it to get my bat on the ball, to make contact. I was taking my swings. But at that point I figured that was the most I could hope for. I began to believe things would get better as I went along. One night as I was going out to dinner with Rico I told him, I thought my swing was almost back. "I think I'm gonna make it back, Rico. I really do," I told him. "I feel my old swing is almost back to where it was."

"I know, kid," he said. "You're looking good. Keep swinging the way you are. You'll hit one out one of these days and you'll be all right." I believed it. I really did, even though I wasn't seeing the ball as well as before. After two weeks of spring training I felt ready to start the season.

The only trouble was there was still more than a couple of weeks to go, and about this time things began to change. I don't know exactly when, but I was aware of a definite change for the worse in my eye. We went into St. Petersburg for a game with the Cardinals. I started and had a really bad game, striking out twice. I know I didn't see the ball at all when it got to home plate. Then I came up in the ninth with the score 2–1 in their favor and I hit a double off Steve Carlton that went over the centerfielder's head. Williams figured I'd had enough for the day and sent George Spriggs in to run for me. As I trotted off the field I got a standing cheer from the fans and I should have been feeling pretty good about the hit. The only thing was it was a lucky hit. I guessed where the ball was going to be. I guessed because I hadn't seen Carlton's previous pitch. On the next pitch I was just looking for it on the outside. If he had tried to brush me back he could have killed me. I wouldn't have seen it coming in time.

A couple of days later I was sitting on the bench next to Ken Harrelson. We had become pretty close friends over the winter and I knew I could trust him. I said to him, "Hey, do you see that light pole over there by third base?" He looked at it and said, "Sure. Why?"

"Because I can't see the light on top of it," I said.

He gave me the eye and said, "Come on, Tony. You're just feeling a little down."

"No, Ken," I said. "I really can't see it, and I should be able to." He argued with me and I couldn't seem to convince him. He thought I needed some cheering up so he took me out to dinner that night. I told him again, "I can't see out of my left eye. It's getting worse all the time. If this keeps up, I'll never play again." I could see his face get serious, but I also knew he didn't really believe me.

It got very depressing. All I had thought of since reporting to Winter Haven was making a comeback and playing ball again. I didn't miss curfews. I stayed away from girls. I watched myself. Only the guys on the club who I was close to and the way I felt inside made trying to come back worthwhile. My father had gone home, and I began to feel more closed off from people than ever.

Now the pitchers were really beginning to make me look bad. Most of the time they threw it right down the middle and I was swinging and missing the ball by a couple of feet. They were throwing the fastball past me and I was swinging late on it. It's pretty frustrating when you know you're a damned good fastball hitter and you can't get your bat on it. I hadn't been bothered too much by headaches, but now they started coming more frequently. I figured it was due to all the pressure I felt. I was straining hard to see the ball, and was still missing. It was pretty hard to take. One day after we played an exhibition with the Braves, we went back to our rooms and I said to Rico, "I can't see the ball right. Something's gone wrong with my eye."

Rico told me that when I was at the plate I leaned away from the pitches and maybe that's why I wasn't seeing the ball too well. But I told him no, that wasn't the reason; I just couldn't see the ball the way I used to.

Williams had told me to take all the extra batting practice I wanted. So one day I asked for some extra hitting and they told me Jerry Stephenson would pitch to me on one of the diamonds. I went out there, waited for about forty-five minutes, and nobody showed up. I walked all the way back and when I got into the clubhouse everybody was gone. The next day I asked our pitching coach, Darrell Johnson, what was going on. "Oh, Stephenson had a sore arm," he said. And I answered, "Well, thanks a lot for telling me."

Another time while we were taking hitting practice before a game at West Palm Beach, Williams was standing behind the cage and said to me, "Aren't you taking too many swings?" I turned around and looked at him. "I'm trying to hit the ball," I told him. "That's all. I'm trying to work things out." "How many goddamned swings are you supposed to take here?" he said and walked away. I was so angry that I took two more swings, threw my bat against the cage and ran around the bases as I was supposed to. I tried to ignore Williams, but it seemed every time I had anything to say to him he just steamed me off all the more.

In a winning game against the Orioles on Friday, March 29, I got a single in the seventh inning and Santiago hit a homer. It was the last hit I got that season. The next day things got worse. We were scheduled to play the Yankees at Winter Haven and I remember feeling bad that day. I had a sore throat. Before the game I played some pepper. I'd throw the ball at Dalton Jones and he'd hit it back at me, but the ball now bounced up and hit me right in the shin. It's always a big joke when you get hit in the shin in pepper, and everybody laughed. But they didn't know what had happened. I wasn't able to follow the ball anymore; I just couldn't measure the speed after it came off the grass. I immediately had to get away from the game because I'd look like a fool. I knew I was in trouble.

My throat was killing me and I went back to the clubhouse. I said to Buddy LeRoux, "I don't think I can play today. I've got this bad throat." Dick Williams had said all along that I could do anything I wanted all spring; he was playing me a lot more than I wanted to play, but I didn't want to say anything. I didn't want to sound like a crybaby. Buddy went and told Dick about my throat. I was sitting by my locker sweating and having the chills when Mike Andrews came up to me and said, "Tony, the game's about ready to start. You ready?"

"Ready? I'm not playing." I told him. "Look at me. I'm sick."

"But your name's in the lineup," Andrews said. I couldn't believe it. I had to run right from the clubhouse all the way out to right field. I didn't even have time to go to the bench.

Jim Bouton was pitching for the Yankees and he wasn't throwing well that day. Yet I struck out four times. I was sick to my stomach. When I took right field after I struck out for the third

73

time I was crying, because I realized I couldn't see the ball. I didn't even know how dangerous the situation was. People were watching me strike out, but only I knew that I was all done. As I walked to the outfield with Yaz I said to him, "I can't see the ball anymore. It's a dark spot and I can't see the ball." Yaz looked at me and said, "Maybe it's just a bad day Tony. You gotta stay in there."

That night Rico came into the room where he saw me sulking. I was pacing the floor. The TV was on but I wasn't watching it. I was in a fog; my headache was with me; I was slowly dying inside.

"Come on Tony, let's go over to Christy's and have a drink," he said.

"No," I said. "I don't want to go anywhere."

"Come on," he said. "It'll do you some good. It won't do you any good moping around the room."

I told him no. I wanted to be left alone. But Rico kept on insisting and I finally said all right, just to get him off my back.

There aren't too many places to get a drink in Winter Haven, and Christy's is where most of the writers and ballplayers hang out. Rico and I joined Danny Osinski at the bar. Danny had a lot on his mind, too. He wasn't sure the club would keep him and he kept waiting for word every day. Rico suggested I have a drink, but I said no, I didn't want any. I didn't even know why I was standing at the bar anyway. But here I was. Gene Oliver finally ordered a beer for me and I barely touched it. It stood there on the bar going flat while I saw my baseball career going out the window. There was talk but I wasn't part of it. I don't know what anybody said, but when I noticed it was almost eleven-thirty I told Rico, "Come on, let's get out of here. Curfew's in half an hour. After striking out four times today I don't want to give anyone the chance to say they saw me in a bar last night boozing it up." We went back to the room.

I hardly slept at all that night and the next morning my throat still felt lousy. I couldn't see taking the bus trip to Orlando so I called the ballpark and our trainer, Buddy LeRoux, answered the phone. "Buddy," I said, "I got a real bad sore throat. I don't think I can make the trip today. Is Williams there?"

"Yeah, he's right here," Buddy said. "Wait a second. I'll tell him." I could hear Buddy tell Williams I was on the phone and had a bad throat. And then I could hear Williams' voice, "If he'd spend more time out of those barrooms he'd be a pretty good ballplayer."

When I heard that I went insane. I said, "Buddy, put that guy on the phone. I want to talk to him. I'm going to come down there and kill him, get him on the phone."

I heard Buddy say, "Hey Dick, Tony wants to talk to you." And then I heard Williams say, "I don't want to talk to him. We did it without him last year, and we'll do it without him this year."

"Buddy, put that bastard on the phone," I shouted. But Williams wouldn't talk to me.

"Buddy," I said. "I'm coming down and I'm going to beat the shit out of him."

Buddy kept his cool. "Stay in your room. I'll be right over," he said.

But I didn't care what Buddy said. I slammed down the receiver and started to get dressed. I was heading for the ballpark. Just as I got to the door—less than a minute after the phone call, Buddy showed up.

7 5

"Look kid. Calm yourself down. If you go to the park now you're only going to make things worse. Here. Take some of this stuff. It'll do your throat good."

"But, Buddy," I said. "It's not the throat. Don't you understand. I can't see!"

He looked up at me. "We ought to tell somebody," he said.

"I know," I answered. "It ain't getting any better. Maybe you ought to tell Dick O'Connell."

Buddy said he'd take care of it.

The next day we had a game with the Braves and before leaving for West Palm Beach I talked to Dick O'Connell. "I have to go back to Boston this week for an Army Reserve meeting," I told him. "I'd like to have the eye checked out while I'm back there."

"Good idea," O'Connel said. "Why don't you fly back tomorrow after our game with the Senators?"

I agreed. I almost felt relieved. Maybe if I went back they'd find out what was wrong and maybe they'd give me something to get that dark spot out of my eye.

I played the game against the Braves and struck out my last time up. I was stunned now; I couldn't see a thing. Yaz came up to me in the clubhouse after the game. "Something wrong?" he said.

"It's no good, Yaz. My eye . . ." I said. I could barely talk. "I'm going back to Boston tomorrow for a Reserve meeting. I'm going to have the eye looked at." Carl shook his head. There was nothing he could say.

We went to Pompano Beach the next day to play the Senators. I was told I'd play six innings, then could leave to catch my ride to Miami and the flight home. Phil Ortega struck me out twice. He got me swinging the first time, then got a three-two changeup that I just looked at. I had one more lick in the sixth inning. Frank Bertaina, a lefty, was on the mound. I was praying now for something, anything. *Just let me hit it,* I said to myself. *Please. Just a little piece of the ball, anything.* As I stepped in I made a cross with my bat on home plate.

Bertaina threw me a changeup on the outside. I swung and missed. The next pitch was high for a ball. Then he threw me a fastball, waist high and down the middle, and I stood there and took it for a strike. I was afraid to swing at it because I didn't see it. All I heard was the pop in the catcher's mitt. Next he threw me a fastball on the outside. I swung and missed by a foot. I stood frozen at the plate for a moment. I was afraid to move. I had never felt so low and beaten in my whole life. I had just struck out for the eighth time in my last 10 at-bats. I dropped the bat right there on top of home plate, then flipped my helmet after it. I turned and ran for the clubhouse, not saying a word to anyone.

When I got there it was empty. I picked up a chair and heaved it against a wall. I began tearing at things, ripping clothes out of lockers, throwing anything that wasn't nailed down. Tears were streaming out of my eyes. I stood there in the middle of the room and said in a loud voice to nobody, "My whole career is gone." I was through. I knew it. I didn't have to have any doctors tell me.

After I showered and dressed someone drove me to the airport in Miami. When I got there I had plenty of time to hang around waiting for the flight. I'm glad nobody recognized me, until it was time to get on the plane. Then some Bostonians recognized me. "Isn't the team still in Florida?" a guy asked me.

"Yeah," I told him. "But I have to go back to Boston for a Reserve meeting. But I'll rejoin the team in Louisville later in

77

the week." I walked on ahead and buried myself in a seat. When the stewardess came around with dinner I told her, "Nothing for me." I wasn't hungry, and besides, I knew my parents would be waiting at Logan Airport for me and we'd go out to dinner later. Then I went to sleep.

When the plane arrived I found my folks, my brother Richie, a girl named Donna Chaves, a real fine girl I am close to, and my Uncle Vinnie and his wife, Phyllis. I was also met by a gang of reporters that made it look like they were waiting for Lyndon Johnson. Somehow, they'd gotten wind of the fact I was coming back and were waiting for me when I got there. I didn't want to tell them anything so when the writers asked what I was doing back there I told them about the Reserve meeting.

"What about the eye?" one guy asked. "How is it? Haven't you been striking out a lot lately?" Sometimes they ask just the right questions.

"That's true," I told him. "It's just one of those things. I've been bothered by headaches the last couple of weeks during games. I guess it's the brightness of the Florida sun. It's that terrible glare that bothers me when I'm hitting. Maybe when we get into regulation parks next week when the season starts the trouble will clear up. I sure hope so."

I was practically biting my tongue when I said those things, but I couldn't let on to anybody what was really happening. As soon as we got away from the reporters my father took me aside and said, "You can't see, can you?"

"You're right, dad," I said.

"Why didn't you tell us when we were down there?"

"I didn't want to upset your vacation," I told him. "Besides, I thought it would clear up. I didn't know it was going to get worse down there." I didn't want to say any more. I could see he was worried enough already and I didn't want to tell my father that I was afraid it might be hopeless now. I just told him I was going to see the doctor while I was in Boston and that I'd probably rejoin the team in Louisville on Friday.

We all went out to an Italian restaurant and had a pizza dinner. With all those people around we didn't discuss the eye too much or talk much baseball. Later on we all drove back to Swampscott and sat around the house for a while and talked. Then I had to take Donna home. My car was down in Florida so I borrowed Billy's. "I'll stay here tonight. See you when I get back, Ma," I said.

Donna lived in Somerville and by the time I got her home it was pretty late. It must have been about one-thirty in the morning as I started for home. The streets of Somerville were deserted. Suddenly, a car came out of nowhere and rammed into me from the side; it had gone right through a stop sign. I was knocked out for about a minute and dazed for several minutes after that. My head hurt. As I sat there in my brother's wrecked car I said to myself, "What next?"

At first I found I couldn't move my legs, and my right eye was now blurred. The police arrived a few minutes later and found me still inside the car. "My legs hurt," I told them. I was pretty shaky. They sent for an ambulance and checked out the other car. The people in the other car turned out to be four underage kids, two boys and two girls. They had been drinking, the car didn't belong to them, and none of them had a license, registration or insurance. Later on the kids tried to sue me for $50,000, but the police knew them. They'd been in trouble before, and I was cleared of any responsibility in the crash.

When the ambulance came I was put in it and taken to Somerville Hospital, where I was wheeled in on my stomach. The night doctor there was a woman and she took X-rays and gave me an examination. She said it didn't appear that I had any severe injuries, just some slight shock and body bruises and bumps, which had given me a headache. She released me. I couldn't go back to Swampscott now, so the Somerville cops offered to drive me back to my own apartment in Kenmore Square.

As soon as I was in my own place I phoned Dr. Tierney. He told me to stay in bed and come see him after I've had a good rest. He also told me I better skip the Reserve meeting the next night and he felt sure I'd be excused because of the accident. I threw up all night. I couldn't sleep and my head hurt. I really thought at this point that I was a marked man. Maybe I wasn't meant to play ball anymore.

Next afternoon I went over to Dr. Tierney's office in Brookline. He gave me a thorough goingover and found no serious injury from the crash other than the fact I had been shaken up and had a bruised shoulder. I'm lucky my folks didn't find out about the crash till morning; otherwise, I'd have my father running into Boston at one o'clock in the morning to see how I was. He heard it on the radio when he was having breakfast the next morning.

After leaving Dr. Tierney I went back to Swampscott where I spent the night. I prayed that night. *Please*, I said. *Let it be all right. Make it all right.* The next day my father took off from work to go to the Retina Associates with me. When we got to Dr. Regan's office they put me through another long series of tests. I read the eye chart. I was given the slit lamp test again. My eye was dilated and a special contact lens was put in so they could look into my eye through a double-lens microscope and see all the way back through my eye. Several people examined me. I went from one tiny room to another, as each of the people ran me through a series of tests. My father watched and I said very little if anything. But watching their faces as I had watched them so many times before I could see things were not good. Molly wasn't even trying to cheer me up this time.

After a while Dr. Regan came over and told us to take a break. "We want to analyze what these tests show," he said. But I could see from the expression on his face what the tests already had shown him: the eye was gone. I could see that, even if he wasn't admitting it just yet. My father could see it too, but he kept his silence as I did.

"Come on outside," my father said to me in a quiet voice. "I want to show you something." When we were alone in the car he said, "Look, there are reporters all over the place and you're gonna see this sooner or later, so you might as well see it now." He took out a folded newspaper he had hidden away and showed it to me. It was a copy of the *Herald Traveler* and it was opened to the sports page. The headline read: "Dick doubts Tony's tale." The story had been written the day before in Winter Haven and it quoted Williams as saying, "I don't think there is anything the matter with Tony's vision despite what he said when he got to Boston last night." Later on in the story Williams said, "If Tony can't get the job done, well, we'll take it from there. We did after August 18 last year. I just might platoon out there. That's what we did last year and I seem to recall we did fairly well the rest of the season without Tony."

The words ate into my flesh. Oh, I hated him at that moment. My baseball career was going out the window and he was saying there was nothing wrong with my eye. Of all the things he had done to get me mad this was the worst, a real cheap shot. "Now take it easy," my father said. "I just wanted you to see it before the writers asked you about it. Okay?"

"Sure," I said. "Come on, let's go." Out in the courtyard we were met by a bunch of writers who had been looking for us all over the grounds. "How's the eye, Tony?" they asked. "What do the doctors say?"

I decided to try and bluff my way through, but I don't think I did a very good job. They could see it in our faces. "We don't know a thing yet," I told them. "They still have to take more tests. We have to come back at two o'clock. We'll find out later." I don't think I fooled any of them. They only had to look at my father's face to know the truth. He was on the verge of breaking into tears.

One of the writers asked me about the Williams quotes in the *Traveler*. I swallowed and said, "I thought Dick was a baseball manager. I didn't know he was an eye doctor, too."

We left and went back to Dr. Regan's office. His face hadn't changed its expression since we'd left. Not that you can really read anything in his face. I swear doctors must take a course in school on how not to reveal what they're thinking. It's the patients who try to find some hidden meaning when they're up tight. Dr. Regan said he wanted another opinion and called in his associate, Dr. Robert Brockhurst, to have a look, too. He put me through the same tests I had gone through before the break and it really got on my nerves. But I didn't say much because I knew how hard they were trying to be sure about the eye.

Finally, Dr. Regan sat my father and me down in his office. "I don't want to be cruel, and there's no way of telling you this in a nice way," he began, "but it's not safe for you to play ball anymore." He then explained very carefully that my eye had grown worse since the last exam in November and that it looked like it was still deteriorating. He said it looked like the cyst had burst while I was down in Florida and that's why I suddenly lost the ball and began striking out so much. When the cyst burst this left a hole in the eye. He said it was like taking a piece of film and burning a hole in the middle of it with a lighted cigarette. The edges around the hole consisted of scar tissue, so even if he could sew up the hole he'd only be putting scar tissue on top of scar tissue and making my eyesight even worse. He told us the ironic part of it was that if the damage were just a millimeter from the center of the eye, I wouldn't have had any trouble picking out the ball.

Then he told us that it wasn't just a question of playing ball; the tissue holding the front wall of the cyst was very weak and that any exercise could cause it to break completely and then I'd have a detached retina. That would require surgery. I couldn't even jog around the block because it might bring on a detached retina. He explained that the last time he had seen me the eye had become stabilized and that if it had stayed that way I probably would still be playing ball. But the condition had deteriorated and my vision in the left eye now was 20/300, which meant I was legally blind in that eye.

My father spoke up. "Could you take my eye out and put it in him?" he asked. Dr. Regan just looked at him without answering. I wanted to cry but I wouldn't because my father was there, and I knew he was holding back his tears for my sake. As my father and I got up to leave I saw Molly in the corridor. She looked about as bad as I felt.

On the drive home my father said to me, "It's not the end of the world, Tony. You're gonna have to start all over in another field." I just stared out the window and didn't say a thing. I was trying to not even think. When we got back to Swampscott my

8 3

mother was waiting for us at the door. She looked at us without saying anything and I just walked past her and headed for my room. As I got to the top step I heard my father say to her, "He's all through."

It had been agreed back in Dr Regan's office for me not to say anything to the press. My father was going to phone Dick O'Connell and the team would announce my retirement. I stayed in my room alone for most of the day. When I came out I didn't say anything to anyone. I heard Richie come back from school and heard them tell him what happened. I know how much he loves me and it killed me to see him take it so bad. He's very much like me—more so than Billy—which means he stays to himself a lot, but inwardly is a happy guy. But this seemed to kill him inside. Later on they phoned Billy in Ocala, Florida, and I could hear my father explaining it to him very quietly.

Later that night my lawyer, Joe Tauro, came over to the house. He'd been a good friend for many years. He was there in the house with me and my father the day I signed my first contract back in September of 1962. He'd shared all the good times and now he had come over to try and help out in bad times. He took me inside a room and said, "Look Tony, you can cry today. But not tomorrow." That's all he said. Then Joe helped me put together my own statement for the newspapers. It went like this:

There are those that tell me I've had a tough break, and I guess I have. But despite it all, I still feel that I'm a lucky guy. I've had an opportunity to realize my lifetime ambition to be a big league ballplayer and to play with the greatest bunch of guys in the world.

Most important, I've been blessed with a wonderful family and great friends who have stuck with me during good days and bad. This is one of the bad days and I can't begin to explain how much it means to me to have the prayers and good wishes of so many good people.

This is what is important to me and I want all these friends to know that I'm not going to quit and that somehow, some way, there will be good days again.

By Saturday the whole world knew I was through. The phone rang constantly with people wanting to talk to me. My mother told them I was in no condition to talk to anyone, but she'd give me the message. When people like family and neighborhood friends came to the house I ran to my room. I wouldn't see anybody; I ate my meals with the family in silence; I watched TV. My parents finally gave up trying to reach me and maybe this helped. At least I was being left alone. During this time I traced all the things that had happened to me and I realized I had been pretty lucky—lucky to have done all the things I had done. I was only twenty-three. I'd have to find something else to do. I didn't know what and I think I enjoyed letting wild things run through my mind. I'd come back as a pitcher and be greater than Sandy Koufax. I thought of going into show business on a full-time basis. I thought of becoming a sports announcer. But I certainly was in no condition to make any decisions. My father kept trying to help, finally getting me to go to a driving range with him where we hit some golf balls.

The first weekend was miserable. On TV one of the stations showed old film clips of me in action with the Red Sox. They had the first home run I ever hit, on the first pitch I ever saw on opening day at Fenway Park in 1964. My mother sat there watching it and crying to herself. I heard my father tell her, "I know it's going to get worse yet. Wait till the games start and he sees them on television. What's going to happen then?"

85

I'm not going to Fenway Park this season, I told myself. *I'm going to be so busy this summer it'll make everybody's head swim.*

On Monday when the team came back to Boston, Rico was at the house as soon as he dropped his bags at his own place. He was great, and it was great just seeing him. He tried not to get too serious, filled me in on the club and tried to get me to relax and smile a bit. We had a few laughs, Rico and me and my parents all sitting around the big table in the kitchen. At one point my mother said, "Tony, have you thought of becoming a left-handed hitter? Maybe you could see the ball better from the other side."

"Ma, you don't understand," I told her. "I can't do that. It would take me years to develop a lefty swing. I have a grooved right-handed swing and that's that." I was awfully easy to live with.

After that gifts and letters and written prayers came in the mail by the sackload every day. I still have no idea how many people actually reached me and how they even knew the address. But every day for weeks the mail would bring religious articles of every faith, gifts, thoughtful sayings, some people even offering me their own eyes. Unbelievable. One woman sent me some holy water she got from Lourdes. I got Jewish blessings from some nice woman I had met when I was at Grossinger's. A priest I never met came to the door. We heard of thousands of masses being said for me. My mother took care of answering these people. She was fantastic at a time when I couldn't do much more than get out of bed in the morning. If anybody in the whole world believed I would ever come back that person was my mother. "If prayers will help," I heard her tell somebody one day, "he'll get better. There must be a God. You remember what Tony said in the statement he released to the press, that

86

somehow there will be good days again? Well, I know he's going to have good days again. I know he is."

I saw only one game at Fenway Park in 1968. The only reason I went was to receive an award from Governor Volpe of Massachusetts for courage and sportsmanship. Otherwise, I'd never have gone. They invited my mother and father to attend with me; we only stayed four innings. The toughest thing I had to do was stand there during the playing of the National Anthem and keep from crying. I looked over at my mother and father and saw how watery their eyes were and I knew then that it was hurting them just as much as it was hurting me. By the time I left my insides were all knotted up. When I took the plaque from the Governor I said to the crowd, "I hope to see you at Fenway Park next year." And then I hurried down the dugout steps.

I managed to keep busy but I was a nervous wreck. I couldn't sit still and I forgot how to talk to people. The season was on, and the Sox weren't doing too well. So on days they were away, I'd go down to the park and I'd leave notes in Ken Harrelson's locker and in Rico's. Nothing big, just little notes to encourage them and the rest of the guys. The clubhouse boys would be there, Moe and the others, and they'd try talking to me like always. They're good kids and I could see on their faces how they felt.

It's crazy, I know, but without baseball I couldn't find a single thing that interested me. I'd once had a pretty fair thing going as a rock singer. Now I got offers to sing at O'Dee's in Cambridge again, and Merv Griffin had called the minute he'd heard about the eye to tell me I could go on his show anytime I wanted, sing or no sing. You'd think I'd grab at these things and turn my

back on baseball. Well, I couldn't. Why? Because without baseball none of these things meant anything to me. I never could
have predicted that, but that's the way it was. Singing in front
of an audience was only fun when it was part of baseball. Without baseball nothing meant anything to me. I needed baseball
to make my life work.

But I had to get my mind off baseball and I finally was persuaded to put together a new nightclub act and play a few dates
at O'Dee's. I got a singer, Cheryl Ann Parker from Revere, an
organ player, a drummer, bass guitar, lead guitar, two trumpets,
a saxaphone, and a trombone. We created a pretty good rock
show, but my heart really wasn't in it. I had worked hard at
singing even though I never took a voice lesson, and I figured
with all that brass behind me they couldn't hear me anyway.

Opening night at O'Dee's was exciting, but when the announcer
said, "And here he is, Tony Conigliaro . . ." I wished he'd been
saying, "And now, playing right field. . . ." When they heard my
name there was cheering from about ninety-five percent of the
people, but there are always a few who try to make your life more
miserable by heckling and booing, and these always seem to be
guys dressed up in half-decent suits and a pair of white sweat
socks with a red or blue ring around the top.

I never really let these guys bother me because I knew how
many people were really behind me; a lot of my friends showed
up at the club to hear me and encourage me. I still had a few
friends I could count on. I had lost a lot of them who I thought
were friends after the doctor's verdict; they didn't need me anymore. But in a way I'm glad this happened. I realize more now
that everybody can't be your friend, and so I admire more the
people who stuck by me in my tragedy. This thing changed
me. Before I was always anxious to meet people, go to parties,

and just have a good time; but all of a sudden I became a loner, only hanging around with my family and exceptionally close friends like Tony Athanas, Jr., my roommate, who stayed by me all the way.

I thought I could stand anything by now. But one night while singing—and I thought I was putting on one of my better shows—I heard some guy yell out, "It's a good thing he can sing, because he can't see." I usually let such remarks pass, but when I heard this I looked around and tried to find the guy who said it. Luckily for me—or him—I couldn't find him. I made a fool of myself, yelling out, "Who said that? Who said that?" There was no answer so I guess he had no guts.

It was June now and while I accepted the fact that my career as a hitter was all over, I felt I could come back as a pitcher. I'd been a good pitcher in high school and I thought if I went to Florida to work out, maybe by 1969 I could be back with the Red Sox as a pitcher. I had talked that spring with Haywood Sullivan, our player personnel director, about what I was going to do. He told me the organization would do anything it could to help me. They already had told me they were going to pay me my full salary for the year and they arranged with the Commissioner's office for me to get full credit for the year so I'd have the five years I needed toward my pension. But Sullivan said to me, "Look, you're in no condition now to make up your mind about such a thing. Let's both think about it for a while, and when you feel you know what you really want to do, just let me know."

Well, now I knew. In spite of all the offers in other fields, it was still baseball: I wanted to become a pitcher. Dr. Regan had told me back in April that I couldn't do as much as jog around the block because he was afraid of a detached retina.

So the first thing I decided to do was call Dr. Regan and ask for another examination. I knew there wasn't a thing I could do without his okay.

I don't think I was as nervous for this examination as for any of the previous ones, because I had come to accept the fact I was through in baseball. The people at the Retina Associates were happy to see me again. We talked for a while and Dr. Regan finally said, "All right, let's have a look." They ran me through the same series of tests and checked each one against my previous tests. Molly never did have a poker face, and I thought I saw something in her expression to give me some cause for hope. When it was over Dr. Regan told me the sight in my left eye had improved to 20/100 from the 20/300 it had been the last time.

"How come?" I asked.

"I really can't say," he told me. "What I can tell you is this—you have not developed a detachment of the retina and it doesn't appear as if you will now. That's healing. In fact, an entire healing process seems to be taking place, which is why your vision in the eye has improved." Then he gave me the words I never thought I'd ever hear again. "I can see no reason why you can't begin working out again," he said. Of course, he told me this didn't mean I was back in baseball again, but the danger of a detached retina seemed to be gone and I could at least try pitching.

The next morning I was down on the beach running. I never thought such a thing would make me so happy; it felt good just being able to run again. Because the club was at home, I didn't get out to Fenway for another week. The papers had got hold of the story and I told everyone not to expect too much; all the doctors had told me was that I could begin working out again. The first day at Fenway it rained and the field was muddy. The ground crew had covered the infield with canvas, but I showed up anyway and worked out for about forty-five minutes. Mostly I ran in the outfield to get my legs strong again.

Then I decided to have a game of pepper with the clubhouse kids. "Come on," I told them. "I'll give each of you five dollars if you can get thirty in a row." They laughed and said that would be easy, especially with me hitting the ball. So they lined up, about three or four of them, and each guy would throw me the ball and I'd slap it back at him trying to get it as close to his feet as possible. If you know how pepper is played you know the ball has to be hit to each kid in order; he's got to field it cleanly and then fire it into me. Well, they'd get to twenty-nine and then one of the kids would blunder. As soon as he did we'd crack up.

The next time I went back I asked Moe to pitch batting practice to me. After hitting a couple of shots I said to him, "Tell you what, Moe, I'll hit three singles on your next three pitches." He said okay, went into his windup and threw me a changeup. I swung and missed, It surprised me. "That was a good pitch," I told him. "But I'm going to remember it. Next time you throw it to me I'm really going to nail it."

Well, he threw me curves and sliders and what passed for his fastball after that, I hit some good shots. Then he threw me that changeup again, and I swung and hit this ball about as good as anybody can hit a baseball. Moe just looked around and watched it sail over the screen in left-center. "That ball won't come down in Kenmore Square for days," he said, and we both laughed. It felt good to laugh; it felt good to hit a ball that well.

Toward the end of the season Mr. Yawkey called me up to his

91

office. The club was on the road and he wanted to know how everything was with me. He assured me the club would help in any way it could. "You know, you'll always have a job with the Red Sox," he told me. I told him that I was thinking of accepting a good offer from Channel 5 in Boston to do TV sports work. I told them I was pleased by the offer, but I wanted to see if I could make it back as a pitcher first. Mr. Yawkey said he was very happy things were going to work out again for me. And then he said, "Tony, I'd like you to do me a favor. Rico Petrocelli was up here the other day and he's got his mind made up he wants to quit baseball. I know how friendly you are with Rico and I think if you talked to him you might help him stay in baseball."

I knew Rico had already talked to Elsie, his wife, and she seemed convinced he was going to quit, too. In fact, Elsie had called me a couple of times and asked me to talk to Rico. But he was still convinced at that time that he wanted to spend more time with his wife, whom he loves deeply, and his kids. He also was unhappy with the fact that his arm had bothered him and that he wasn't being played the last three weeks. Rico also told me that without me and Mike Ryan (who had been traded to the Phillies) he really wasn't close to anybody on the club and at times he got depressed. He had been offered an excellent contract from Kelly's Hamburg Company and he already had done several TV commercials and some public relations work for them. Rico felt that he could make good money with Kelly and be around his family more often.

I tried to explain to Rico that he would really miss the game once he was not around it, even though so many things bothered him. I told Rico how much I disliked a lot of the things about baseball too, but once it was taken away from me a big piece of my life was missing. He said, "That's different. You don't have a wife and kids." I tried to explain to him that he could make more money in baseball in a short period of time than he could selling hamburgers. I told him to stick out the year, and I'd be back in the big leagues with him next year, pitching.

Dick O'Connell and Haywood Sullivan had been coming out to the park whenever I worked out. They had seen me throw at Fenway and told me if I wanted to go Sarasota and try to make it back as a pitcher it was okay with them. So in November I went down to Sarasota, where the Red Sox had a team in the Winter Instructional League. The teams in this league are composed mostly of kids just starting on their way up, but top pros in the organization work with them. It's also where big-leaguers who have problems to work out will go. Billy Gardner, who had been a good major-league infielder, was running the team, assisted by Mace Brown, an oldtime major-league pitcher, and Bots Nekola, the scout who signed Yaz.

As soon as I got there, I told Gardner I came down to be a pitcher and nothing else. He said, "Okay, let's go to work." I spent the first day throwing lightly and doing a little running. I met the kids on the club, got a uniform, and later found a place to live in Lido Beach. The kids looked up to me for what I had done in the big leagues, so they asked many questions, especially a good-looking kid named Dennis Gilbert from California. From the time I got there till the day I left I loved talking about hitting and I did everything possible to help these kids. I worked with them in the batting cage and I gave help to anybody who asked for it.

But at the same time I was still serious about becoming a big-league pitcher in a hurry. I already had a taste of minor-league life in Wellsville and I didn't like it. So I knew if I

93

was going to make it I'd want to make it *without* having to go back to the minors. For the first week or so I just threw on the sidelines; I went through some of the mound drills and I soon developed a sore arm. About the eighth day I pitched batting practice. Later Gardner asked me if I wanted to get in the cage and hit a few balls myself. I told him I might as well "because I'm going to have to hit if I'm going to pitch."

I went to the bat rack to get a bat. When I was a hitter I used to grab that bat, I couldn't wait to get my hands on it. But I didn't feel that way now. The next thing I did was find a helmet with a flap on the left side, and as I stepped into the cage I was thinking of that horrible accident I had August 18, 1967. I stepped in with absolutely no confidence, a little afraid of being hit. But I knew that the pitcher had good control and was just going to throw the ball down the middle. I looked at the first pitch that came in and let it go because it was outside. I guessed the pitcher was afraid of hitting me. Probably Billy Gardner had told him to keep the ball away. The second pitch came waist high right down the middle. I didn't swing. I just wanted to see what the ball looked like. The last time I had stepped into a batting cage to hit against a pitcher was three months earlier at Fenway Park. But this time the ball looked clear and I could see the spin.

I dug in now and realized that I had a shot at hitting the ball. The first pitch I swung at I hit a line drive over the second-baseman's head and I think everybody's eyes opened up a little bit. I hit a few more shots like that, fairly hard, but with no real power; I realized that this was the first time I had hit in three months and I felt in time I could get my whole swing back. I didn't want to show the excitement I felt. I knew this guy was

94

only throwing the ball at three-quarter speed. I still told myself I was going to be a pitcher.

Billy Gardner came running up to me and said, "You look great up at the plate. You really hit a couple." I shook my head and said, "No, Billy, you know he's just lobbing the ball in. I just want·to concentrate on pitching." I didn't want Billy getting excited and I didn't want to get too excited myself, because I was thinking that I never wanted to go through again what I went through in spring training in 1968.

Billy said, "All right, just keep pitching. But do me a favor, will you, and take batting practice every day? I'll leave pitchers back here when we go on a trip. I just want you to keep swinging. You're not ready to pitch in a game yet, so take extra hitting whenever you can. But we'll continue to work hard on your pitching." I said okay. I thought maybe Billy was making a bargain with me. He'll continue to work with me as a pitcher, and all he wants me to do is take hitting practice. Of course, I could see what was in the back of his mind; the same thing was in my mind, too. I didn't want to invite anymore heartbreak, but as long as one other person thought there might be a speck of hope, I was ready to go along with him.

The next day I bought a pair of sunglasses for $30. The glare from the sun was bothering me and the glasses really helped. Each day after that I hit the ball a little bit better, seeing it more clearly—but I didn't tell anybody. Every time somebody talked about my hitting, I would change the subject and start talking about pitching. I still wasn't convinced that I could hit game-type pitching. On the fourth day I was encouraged enough to call for a few curve balls. I hit one curve; then I hit the next one. And the one after that. I belted them harder and harder, and finally I sent two balls over the left-center field fence. It was the most beautiful sight in the world.

After practice Billy Gardner called me into his office and said, "Tony, you're going to think I'm crazy, but I want you to give up pitching and try to make it back as an outfielder. I saw you swing a bat while I was on the club with you in '64 and you look close to the way you looked then."

I said, "I don't feel too bad at the plate, Billy. Tomorrow I want to hit without knowing what's coming. Just give me a little more time."

I couldn't sleep that night because I had a load on my mind. I had convinced myself that pitching was going to be my new future, and now all of a sudden, hitting became a possibility again. I thought I was seeing the ball better, but of course, I knew what was coming each time. Now I was going to find out if I could hit something without knowing in advance what it was. *Nobody gets a second chance after an injury like mine,* I'd told myself all along. Now I was going to find out if I'd been wrong. I knew one thing: If there was one chance in the world I could come back as a hitter it was worth a try; no, not just a try, but an all-out effort.

I went to the ballpark the next day tired. I'd been wearing myself out hitting, pitching, and running, and I was mentally tired, too. Because I was due to start my first game in a day or two, my father and my Uncle Vinnie flew down from Boston and were going to stay with me at my apartment in Lido Beach. When I got to the park I found Sam Mele, Mr. Yawkey's superscout, and Frank Malzone were there too. I guess Gardner had told the front office and the scouts were sent down to see what the real story was.

For the first time in a long while I took batting practice without knowing what was coming. I don't think I hit the ball that well. I was a little arm-weary and I had blood blisters all over my hands; and my swinging wasn't that good. After hitting I did a little bit of running in the outfield and left without saying much to anybody. My father and uncle were there, of course, and as we drove away my father said, "You looked good at the plate." When we went out to dinner that night I completely avoided the subject of hitting and talked a lot about my pitching. My father got the idea and didn't press me on the hitting.

The next morning I found out that the three of us had lain awake all night, with our eyes open looking at the ceiling, all thinking about the same thing. When I looked out the window I thought I'd never seen it rain so hard before. We all headed for the ballpark not really thinking there would be a game. The main ballpark in Sarasota was too wet, so the game was moved out to the White Sox practice field. By game time the rain had stopped.

When I went to warm up I was in the right frame of mind. I had hardly talked to anybody. My arm felt good, not great; I wasn't tired anymore; I was all keyed-up. I took the mound in the first inning and kept saying to myself, "I'm going to do it." We were playing Philadelphia, the toughest team in the Winter League. I stepped on the mound and faced the first batter. I got myself mad. My teeth were grinding. The ball felt as if it was no bigger than a golf ball in my hand.

I threw the first pitch low in the dirt. The second pitch was in the same place. Then I threw a fastball for a strike. The first batter popped up, and I retired six in a row.

I was only going to pitch three innings, so my goal was to get my next three batters out. The first man up in the third was my old buddy, Mike Ryan, who was now with the Phillies. Mike had come down to Florida to work on his hitting. Now he had one

97

foot in the box and one foot out and he was laughing like crazy. Tense as I was, I turned around, faced the centerfielder, and burst out laughing. I didn't want the people in the stands to see me laughing; they wouldn't understand. After about two minutes I finally went into my windup. As soon as I got to the top I was smiling again; I just couldn't get serious. I threw a curve to Mike and he hit a wicked line drive about ten feet foul off the screen in left field. Even that couldn't get me serious.

Mike and I are old buddies. We had first met in the Winter League in 1962 and Mike really took care of me. I was seventeen years old and it was my first time away from home. He roomed with me and taught me how to behave, even how to dress. The first time he saw me I had just come down from Boston wearing a DA haircut, a new black suit, and thick white basketball socks. He took one look at me and said, "You gotta be kidding." He was the first guy to straighten me out. We became the best of friends, and this whole situation of pitching to a guy I really knew and liked was too funny for the both of us to handle.

I stepped on the rubber again. By now we were both just smiling. I thought he was expecting a fastball now, so I threw another curve ball and he hit a grounder to third base and was thrown out.

As Mike ran by the mound he said to me, "How the hell did you ever get me out?" I said, "There's been a few guys who have got you out," and then we both laughed. The next guy I got to pop out, and now I needed only one more out to finish my three innings' work. I got two strikes on him with no balls and I wound up walking him. Now I had to pitch from a stretch, something I hadn't worked on very much since going down there. It was very uncomfortable and I walked the next man, too. My first pitch to the next batter was a curve ball and he hit it to the shortstop. Only there was no shortstop: he had run over to cover second base and the ball went into left field. The outfielders were spread around pretty good and by the time the leftfielder came up with the ball the guy who hit it was on third base and there were two runs in. The next guy got a broken-bat single, so I wound up giving three unearned runs in my first game and we lost, 3–0.

Billy Gardner had me leading off the batting order because he wanted to get a good look at me. I walked on a three-and-two pitch that was a slider about three inches off the corner. I found out later that the fact that I could judge the pitch was outside for a ball opened the eyes of Sam Mele and Frank Malzone. My second time up I hit a solid line drive right at the shortstop. Afterwards, I showered, dressed, and left with my father and uncle. I was satisfied with my pitching performance, but I also kept thinking of that line drive to the shortstop. I had got good wood on the ball and hit it hard.

The next day Sam Mele told me I could continue working on my pitching if I wanted to, but the front office had told him they wanted me to work on my hitting and outfielding, too. "Personally, I think you should give up pitching," he said, "but that's up to you." I told Sam I wasn't going to give up pitching, but I'd work as hard as I could on the other things. I knew Billy Gardner wanted me to play the outfield in games I wasn't pitching. So for the next week or so, Sam ran me into the ground, chasing balls, hitting in the cage. I told him I was glad to see him going back to Boston because he was killing me.

The morning after my first game as a pitcher I woke up and my arm felt like it was in a cast. I couldn't bend it; it was swollen and I had torn a muscle around the shoulder area. I tried to pitch in St. Pete four days later and I lost by 2 touchdowns and a field goal. I was bombed for fifteen runs by Minnesota. That wasn't my last game as a pitcher, but maybe it should have been. I pitched against St. Louis at St. Pete, worked 6 innings and gave up 3 runs. I lost that one, too, so now I was 0-3. My arm felt terrible and what made it worse were those line drives that went shooting past by my ear. I decided pitching wasn't that easy.

In a game at Dunedin against Detroit, Dick O'Connell and Dick Williams were in the stands when I hit a double off the fence in left-center field. Later on I hit a hard ground ball up the middle for a base hit. After the game, O'Connell came over and said, "Tony, you look great. We think you can make it back next year." That was the greatest thing I'd heard in all this time. Williams was smiling and said, "I hear you've been doing great down here. Keep up the good work. I want you back in Winter Haven this spring to play right field for me and bat cleanup." Then O'Connell said, "Now we're gonna get out of here because it's too cold. We've seen enough."

I ran out to right field with a feeling of new life. But I still realized it was a long road ahead. As I passed Billy Gardner, I said, "Billy, you were right. I am gonna make it back." He smiled and said, "Tony, throw away that toeplate."

There was more excitement around the house in Swampscott than there had been in some time. The papers were blaring out the news that I was going to try and come back again in 1969, and immediately after I got back from Florida the same old question started up again, "Hey, Tony. How's the eye?" I must have been asked that question 500,000 times, always the same way. I didn't mind it the first 500,000 times, but after that I began to wish they'd at least vary the way they asked.

Of course, I knew I really hadn't proved anything yet. But the whole house had the old ring to it again. I mean my family never lost faith in me, but they were depressed over my being out of baseball. Now the laughing was back and I could see how changed my parents had become. Our family is so close that when something happens to one of us we all suffer just as much as the person who is hurt. My mother and father live and die for the three of us and that's why we have always tried not to get into serious trouble. For that reason I was all the more apprehensive when the Red Sox set up another appointment for me with the retina people. I was afraid it might be the same old story again.

One November day my father took off from work, and we went down there together. They were a little angry with me because I hadn't gone in for an exam before leaving for Florida. They had expected me, but ever since the accident I had my eye examined so many times that it had become a real strain on me. But I was looking forward to this exam because I felt something good might come out of it; it also frightened me because I knew no improvement was supposed to occur.

On the drive down to the Retina Associates my father and I were quiet. All he said was, "I know everything is going to be all right," and I answered, "I hope so." The Red Sox had asked us to keep it from the press—and nobody was happier about that than I was. So when we got there we saw no writers or photographers for the first time since I could remember coming there.

Dr. Regan and the rest of the staff greeted us when we got inside and a couple of minutes later they were working on me all over again. Molly gave me the field test to see what my direct vision was like now. I'd follow a white light across a radar screen with my left eye and press a buzzer whenever I saw another light coming from outside angles. Molly would stop the second light in the center. When I saw the second light leave the center light, I rang the buzzer quickly, which showed her the old blind spot was not there. My father stood behind watching, and I could tell he was praying silently to himself.

I realized after a short while that something funny was going on. I knew I wasn't supposed to see some of the things I was seeing and I sat there with goose pimples growing on my back. I didn't want to get overconfident because I still had several more tests ahead, but for the first time I found myself really looking forward to seeing the results.

When I finally got up Molly had a smile on her face. She'd make a terrible poker player, let me tell you. She said, "I don't believe it," and she ran out of the room to Dr. Regan's office, told him something and then came back. Next she wanted to test me on the eye chart. She put a black patch over my right eye and then projected a large letter on a screen. "Do you see that?" she asked. "Sure," I said, "it's an E."

Then she made it smaller and asked, "Do you see that?" and I said yes. Molly said, "That's funny, you didn't see it the last time." She then projected a group of letters across the screen. I read them across quickly, and I couldn't hear a sound in the room. She then made another group of letters, only smaller, and I kept saying, "Yes, I can read them," and I did accurately. She then got it down to the 20/20 line. I had just read 20/30 and didn't believe it, and now as I read the 20/20 line I couldn't believe it. That meant, miraculously, my vision in the left eye was almost perfect. Molly then flipped another line on at 20/15, but I couldn't read it, but who cared? Tears came into my eyes and I thought how happy my father must be at this point. Molly snapped on the light. Then she dilated my left eye with some drops and said, "Dr. Regan is not going to believe this." Then she ran out of the room.

While she was out of the room my father looked at me and said, "I prayed for this. I can't wait to call your mother." And I said, "Let's finish the tests first," but I didn't say it with my usual depressed tone.

Molly came walking back in. I could see by her face she was even happier than I was, because she had seen me in my worst moment, and I think she realized how much it meant to me to have my sight back again. Dr. Regan followed her in. He wasn't smiling, but then he wasn't frowning, either. "Come on," he said, "let's go in the other room." He wasted no time in setting my chin on a bar and he began looking at my macula. I could feel him breathing on my cheek. He wasn't saying anything, except, "Ah, ha." But finally he said, "You're an amazing young man, and someone must have been saying an awful lot of prayers for you."

"Why?" I asked.

"I can't explain it," he said, "but that large hole you had in your eye is gone, except for a small piece of scar tissue." He then got up, not waiting for my reaction and went to Dr. Brockhurst in the next office. He wanted another opinion. Brockhurst began by looking into the eye. But in a couple of minutes he said to Dr. Regan, "Charley, you dilated the wrong eye. I'm looking into the good one."

"No, I didn't," Dr. Regan said, "that's the eye, all right." Brockhurst shook his head. I backed off the chair. I looked at my father. There was water in his eyes. It was the best I'd seen him look in two years.

Dr. Regan was smiling now. He then tried to explain to me what he figured had happened to the eye since my last visit. The edges of tissue along the inner rim of the hole in the macula had sealed down smoothly along the back wall of the eye. These once sharp and raised edges had healed back in such a way that they had almost disappeared. The only evidence I had been injured was a small pigmentation that most doctors would assume I had been born with. There was almost no scar tissue to be seen. All of this they regarded as remarkable and never could have predicted. Most of my depth of field had returned and with both eyes open, there was no real distortion. The blind spot had gone and the hole had filled with viscous fluid. To me it all said one word: Miracle.

Dr. Regan asked me which of us should tell Dick O'Connell, and I said, "It would sound kind of funny coming from me. Why don't you call him?" He did while we sat there in the office, and after hearing the doctor's story O'Connell told him to put me on. When I got on he congratulated me and I could tell how happy he really was. He told me to rest up, get in shape, and he'd see me before I had to leave for Winter Haven.

When I got through talking to O'Connell I felt like screaming at the top of my lungs, running outside and telling the whole world I could see again. But I had to stay a while longer for a few minor tests and to have a picture taken of my macula. When he was finished Dr. Regan came over to us and shook my hand and my father's hand; there was really nothing for him to say. Dr. Regan showed by his face that he was as happy as we were. Dick O'Connell asked him not to make any announcements to the press, that the ballclub would make a release in the morning.

Before we left the Retina Associates my father said, "Wait a minute. Before we go, I gotta call your mother." He quickly ran to a phone booth. I don't know exactly what he said, but he made it short. We then jumped in the car and went back to Swampscott. My mother was smiling from ear to ear and the whole scene around the house would sound too dramatic to describe, but I'll tell you one thing; at that point all we could think of was, thank God.

By now I knew I needed to get away for a while and take a nice long rest someplace and I decided to go to Hawaii. But first I wanted to see Las Vegas. I'd spend four days there and see Frank Sinatra, Buddy Hackett, Shirley Bassey, and Jose Feliciano. A friend of mine, Elliott Price, arranged to get tickets to see them all at Caesar's Palace. When I got there I met Rocky Marciano, one of my all-time idols. I told him how I'd played ball with one of his brothers in high school. That night I was Rocky's guest as we saw the Sinatra show.

The next night I watched Shirley Bassey and Buddy Hackett. He's always been one of my favorite performers; this night he was electrifying. Wearing a Nehru jacket and some beads around his neck, he said, "Bet your ass I got class," and that broke everybody up. I was sitting up in front by myself and as Hackett got halfway through his act he said to the audience, "Did you ever notice how baseball players are always scratching themselves when they're up at the plate?" Now my eyes opened wide. He said, "There are two big offenders in the American League. One of them is Carl Yastrzemski." The place was breaking up at all this, because he was going through a few motions up there on the stage. "But the biggest offender is Tony Conigliaro." I didn't even know he knew I was there. My heart started pounding when he said, "Any of you ever hear of Tony Conigliaro?" About half the place started applauding. That wasn't bad, I thought. Then Buddy began talking about me and my injury and my comeback attempt earlier that season, giving my average and everything, and then he said, "Would you believe Tony is in our audience tonight? Stand up and let the people get a look at you," he said.

I got up and spotlights were on me and there was genuine clapping that made me feel good, that I wasn't a forgotten ball-player. Buddy then said to me, "Wait, I'm coming down." When he got to me he said in a serious voice, "Tony, I know all about your accident. It was a real tragedy. I've said prayers for you. If Jewish prayers can help I'll do all I can." You could hear a pin drop in the place. There were tears in Buddy Hackett's eyes. I couldn't believe the whole thing was happening. He won me as a friend for lifetime. He went back on stage, continued using my name through his act the rest of the show, got them laughing again and when it was over he said, "This is one of the happiest moments in my life. You people have been great tonight, and Tony, I meant everything I said from the bottom of my heart." He went off and was brought back with a standing ovation.

In Hawaii, I spent my time lying on the beach flat on my back. I'm convinced if I wasn't a ballplayer I could spend my life very easily as a beach bum. About my third day there, I saw a girl in a bikini walk by. She was golden brown and beautiful. As a matter of fact the whole beach faced her way when she walked. Whenever I've seen a beautiful girl that I really liked I've always made an effort to meet her. This girl walked up and sat down at a table in the bar area. I got up and walked over. I didn't know what to say and so I just smiled and said, "Hello." She smiled right back, so I thought it would be all right if I asked if I could sit down. This girl was so beautiful up close that I talked like I had a speech defect. I wasn't pronouncing my words correctly and she wasn't either. I came out and said, "What are you so nervous for?" Then we both smiled and laughed and I ended up dating this girl for the three weeks I stayed.

106

One night we went to a Polynesian restaurant. I hadn't told her I was a baseball player. After dinner the waiter dropped two fortune cookies on the table. Mine read: "This will be the best year you ever had. Make good use of it." I took my wallet out, put this piece of paper in it, and said to myself, maybe this really means something. I'm somewhat superstitious, especially when it comes to baseball. If I get a home run with a particular sweat shirt on I wear it again the next day, no matter what. As a matter of fact, I guess I'm a little extra superstitious about baseball, because I'll even go so far as to eat the same foods and do the same things during a hitting streak.

We had been drinking through dinner and the more the evening ran on the more I felt I had to tell someone about this fortune cookie. So I told the girl I was a baseball player named Tony Conigliaro and all about my injury. She laughed and said, "I feel stupid saying this, but I never heard of you." I knew she really meant it.

But this girl impressed me because I thought for once I was liked by somebody who did not know who I was. I had always feared in the back of my mind that girls go out with me because I'm a ballplayer. I've never really been that sure a girl is out with me just because she likes being with me. That's why I enjoy dates more away from Boston where fewer girls have heard of me.

After three weeks in Hawaii I really wanted to be home again and I flew directly back to Boston in something like ten hours. It was just before Christmas now and the house looked beautiful, all decorated with lights. Everything was so jovial, so different from last year at the same time. I went to bed and when I woke up on Christmas morning I had a case of the flu. The temperature in Boston that day was around six degrees below zero and

the heat wasn't working too well in the house. I had a temperature of 104 degrees and had to walk around the house with a
bathrobe, two pairs of pajamas and a towel wrapped around my
neck. We had sixty-mile-an-hour winds, and I was freezing from
the cold and sweating from my fever.

I complained all day long and my father kept saying, "It's not
that cold in here." I told my father, "What do you mean? We have
twenty-mile-an-hour gusts *inside* the house," and I also said there
were small craft warnings up in the bathtub with intermediate
snow flurries. He grabbed me by the hands and said, "All right
let's go over and take a look at the thermostat and I'll bet you
it's at least sixty-five degrees." We did and I said, "Look at that,
it's forty-two. That's how cold it is."

I received my contract from the Red Sox. They had come
through again. Since I was on the disabled list they could have
cut my salary a full fifteen percent, but they only cut it ten. I was
in no bargaining position, really, and I would have signed a contract if all it called for was a ham sandwich. As I signed it my
father looked over my shoulder and said, "Who would have ever
thought you'd be putting your name down on that beautiful
piece of paper again?" I looked at Richie, whose eyes were
bugging out, and said, "Not bad for an old man of twenty-four,
hey?"

Billy and I had agreed to go to Florida about the middle of
February and spend about two weeks at the Doral Country
Club working out and getting into shape. I also had promised
Billy I'd work on his swing. He was just about ready to make it to
the majors. He's a really great outfielder, but at the plate he
has an in-out swing. This causes him to hit the ball to right-center
field weakly, and I wanted him to build up his wrists and learn

to use a quick downward snap so he'd hit down on the ball, like chopping wood. I wanted him to pull the ball more for distance and I felt sure that if he could develop this new swing in Florida he'd be ready for the big leagues. Sure I realized he'd be competing for an outfield job, maybe even mine, but he's my brother and if I didn't make my comeback I didn't want anyone but Billy to take my place.

Besides, Billy has always been in the background in baseball because of me. He followed me through St. Mary's High School and any time he did anything good they'd always say, "Yeah, but you should have seen his brother Tony do it." I think it's always bothered Billy not to get his name in the papers as much as he should have, but he'd never say anything about it. I know he wants to be great and I'd do anything in my power to help him reach his goal.

We spent two weeks down in the Florida sun playing golf and working out with a bat and a ball. We worked so hard we were both aching. We worked out for two hours every morning, running, fielding, hitting, then we'd have lunch and play some golf. I worked on Billy's swing, and about the fifth day I saw him getting the hang of it. As for me, I could really see the ball now, better than I did a year earlier, and I hungered to get up to Winter Haven. Billy kept on encouraging me, saying, "You look just like you did in 1967."

There was a threat of a ballplayers' strike over pension fund so I didn't get to camp till that was settled. I arrived in Winter Haven about 10:30 P.M. I didn't see anybody and went directly to my room. I had asked Dick O'Connell to room alone. I wanted to concentrate on my comeback, without any distraction.

Next morning I got up around eight o'clock, had breakfast

with Billy and Harrelson, and we drove over to the ballpark about a mile away from the Holiday Inn. How good it was to walk into that clubhouse and see all the guys again. "Hey, T. C., want some help putting your uniform on?" Reggie Smith asked me. Yaz came over and began talking in his rapid way about what a great team we had this year. Russ Gibson said, "Fall River's rooting for you"—that's his hometown. I kept saying to myself, how great if I can just make it to opening day. Jose Tartabull and Rico were there. And there in my locker hung No. 25. Fitzy came over to me and said, "Dick wants to see you in his office." I headed for the manager's office.

Dick got up to shake my hand when I came in. He said, "Look, you're on your own again. We don't want to rush you. You can play in the regular games whenever you want. Just let me know." I told him I didn't want to be treated any differently than anybody else. There's nothing like playing under game conditions I told him, and I wanted to play in the first exhibition game. He agreed. He had nothing else to say to me.

In many ways it was like what I had gone through in 1968. Long days of batting practice, intra-squad games, then the exhibitions started. I was under the same scrutiny and the same pressure all over again. But this spring there was one big difference: I could see the ball.

At first I didn't hit too well, and I struck out often. As we got on in spring training, though, I began making better contact and getting my share of hits. But I still hadn't hit a home run and that bothered me. I had been a power hitter before and I wanted to hit a homer as a sign that I was back. I'd wake up in the morning and the first thing I'd think was, will this be the day I do it? With a week to go in spring training I still hadn't hit a homer.

I had hit four balls well enough to go out of the park, but the wind was against me. It was blowing straight in and the balls were caught by the wall. Just one home run and I'd be happy.

I knew my timing was off after more than a year's layoff. Besides, I was trying to figure out where to stand at the plate. Before I was hit, I was a crowder. Now I stood about a foot back from the plate and was using a 36-inch bat instead of a 34½-inch one to make up for the difference. Gradually as spring training progressed, I began to move closer and closer back till I was five inches away again—where I had always stood.

Finally, on March 27, I defied the wind and hit one over the left-field wall against the Reds at Tampa. What's funny about that day is that the wind was really blowing in from left field. I remember I got mad thinking, why couldn't the wind blow out for a change? During practice no balls were hit out of left field. Harrelson even remarked that there'd be no home runs that day. In the fourth inning Mel Queen pitched me 2 sliders for balls and I figured the fastball would be next. I was ready to be quick and to hit it hard. I was right. I made solid contact and the ball sailed towards left. As I ran toward first base I said to the ball, "Go, go, get the hell out of here." It did. Home runs always thrill me, but this baby really excited my insides. It was my first homer since August 8, 1967, nine days before I got hit. It was a relief to me to finally hit one and I knew the guys on the club were waiting to see me do it. When I got back to the dugout everyone acted like I just hit a World Series homer. "See you in Fenway Park," I told them.

After that I was a lot more relaxed. I was able to sleep; my personality changed; I laughed a lot more. I hit another homer against the Twins on April 2. Then we went into the Astrodome for a four-game series with the Astros. I hit one in the first game, then I hit another one in the fourth game. I wound up the exhibition season playing in 23 of the 26 games, batted .243, with 11 RBI's and a club high of 4 home runs. Now for the first time I believed Dick Williams. I was going to be in right field on opening day.

We were opening the season in Baltimore. Billy had made the club and we decided to share a room. Only one of us got sleep. I must have wakened six or seven times that night. Each time I could hear Billy on the other bed breathing deeply. My night was a crazy mixture of dreams about appearing on the Merv Griffin Show and facing Dave McNally's inside sliders the next day. Once I dreamed I saw Jimmy Durante sitting at a table, and when I went over to say hello to him he disappeared.

The next morning Billy and I had breakfast with a writer named John Devaney who was following me for *Sport* magazine. I stared at my strawberries and bananas till they wilted, while Billy hardly touched his pancakes. No one had very much to say, and I said, "I would eat a lot bigger breakfast normally but I'd like to leave a lot of room for these butterflies to play around in."

Then we headed for the ballpark. There's a strange ritual ballplayers go through on opening day: they get dressed too soon. Usually during a season, a player times himself to be in full uniform just before he has to go work out. But on opening day everybody's in a hurry and maybe just a bit more nervous than at any other time When I got there I said to Harrelson, "You look like a kid twenty-one years old." Even Ken was up tight. He just flushed a little and went on dressing.

When I was dressed in my uniform I pulled out a new glove that I hadn't broken in yet. "Where's your old glove?" somebody asked me. "Last spring I gave all my gloves away," I told him. "I didn't think I'd need one anymore." Then I went out to the field and did some jogging in the outfield before it was time for me to hit. While I was out there I heard a girl calling me. I looked into the stands and a young girl told me she and her friends had hung out a banner reading, "Welcome back Tony C," but the officials had made her tear it down. "Christ," I said to myself, "that wouldn't have hurt anyone. Wouldn't have hurt anyone at all."

All of a sudden the batting cage came down, the ground crew came out to sweep the infield, the umpires came out, they played the Star Spangled Banner and we had a ballgame. Reggie Smith led off with a walk, Mike Andrews singled and Yastrzemski doubled to right field scoring Smith. Harrelson then popped up. As I left the on-deck circle there was a small ripple of applause that seemed to build into a giant wave by the time I stepped into the batter's box. I was glad that I hadn't eaten my breakfast. As McNally started to pitch I told myself to be quick with my hands and do something to thank these people. His first pitch was a fastball that I started to go for, then thought better of, and let it go for a ball. Then he came way outside for ball two. Next he pumped a fastball right at my knees. When the umpire called it a strike I turned around and said, "No, it was inside." But he shook his head and said, "No, it's a strike." I then realized that in the last couple of weeks I'd been moving closer to the plate so that pitches that once looked like balls inside were now really strikes. I fouled the next couple of pitches off, and then McNally gave me that slider I'd been dreaming about and I swung and missed for strike three. I came back to the bench disgusted and realized how nervous I had been.

In the Orioles' half of the first inning Paul Blair hit a deep fly to right-center field which Reggie and I closed in on. It was Reggie's ball, but suddenly I heard him say, "I can't see it. I can't see it."

"Okay," I shouted to him. "I've got it," and I made the catch. Just having the ball slam in my glove got rid of what was left of my butterflies.

My next time up I walked on a close 3–2 pitch, but I *knew* ball four was just outside. By the fifth inning we were leading, 2–1, and Dave Leonhard was pitching for them. I had a 2–2 count and decided to just try and meet the ball. Leonhard gave me a slider and I met it well, smacking it into center field for my first big-league hit in a long time. The Orioles tied the game in the eighth at 2–2 and we went into extra innings.

Pete Richert, a left-hander, was pitching in the tenth. Harrelson led off and reached first on an error. I got the bunt sign and missed on my first try. Richert then threw me a high fastball, and I swung and missed for strike two. *Settle down,* I told myself. *Be quick but not jumpy.* He gave me a waste pitch for ball one, then just missed with a slider on the inside; the umpire almost called it strike three. I'm glad he didn't because I hit Richert's next pitch about as hard and as well as I've ever hit a ball in my life, sending it over the left-field fence for a home run.

My God. I did it, I really did it. I ran the bases as though I was floating. As I rounded second I was grinning like a little boy. In the third-base box Popowski was jumping and yelling, "Hey Tony, hey Tony." All I could yell out was," Oh Pop, oh Pop." When I crossed home plate Boomer Scott was standing there with his hands out and duked me. "What do you think of that, Boomer?" I said. "What do you think of that?" At the dugout the guys were all reaching for me at one time. Billy, Reggie, Rico, Yaz and everybody. They were pounding my back and grabbing me by the shoulders. I was being hugged to death. Even Dick Williams came over and kissed me on the cheek.

I could have bit him in the neck.

PART II

My mother says I was born prematurely and that I've been in a hurry ever since. I was an ugly baby. In fact, my father says I was so scraggly-looking that he joked about wanting to ditch me in a waste basket the first time he saw me. My mother won't admit it now, but she was ashamed to take me out in the carriage. People would come up, and before getting a good look at me, would start to say something nice. Then they'd take a look in the carriage, catch themselves, and stammer something nice anyway. My father would look at my mother and shrug, as if to say who are they kidding.

When I was born on January 7, 1945, my parents were living in Revere, Massachusetts. They had bought a house and were struggling financially. My father worked in a zipper factory, but that was only one of his jobs. He was always trying to make a killing in some business of his own. For example, he decided to go into the music stand business. His brother Joe was playing trombone in Vaughn Monroe's band, so he figured they could start out by selling some stands to Vaughn Monroe.

My father and uncle went down to New York to see Vaughn Monroe. Monroe liked the idea and wanted to put up all the money and take fifty percent of the company. But my father and my uncle were too greedy and said no. They went back to Revere and started building 500 music stands in a shack in the back yard. Vaughn Monroe bought thirty of them but not long after that the big-band business went downhill, and they didn't sell another music stand. The rest of them just grew rusty in the shack.

That shack is the first thing I can remember in this world. I can remember playing inside it when I was about four years old while my father and my Uncles Joe and Guy and a lot of their relatives put together that ridiculous-looking assembly line of wobbly music stands. That was also about the time my father gave me my first ball and bat and started to play with me. I liked to hit right from the start and I'd wear my father out. After that my uncle, Vinnie Martelli, who is my mother's brother, would take over. My father never tried to force baseball on me. Like any father he went out and got me a ball and bat and I happened to like it. My father loved sports but never played baseball himself. He played some softball but in high school he was really more interested in football and track.

During these years my father also ran a doughnut shop called Marty's, short for Martelli's; it was originally owned by my Uncle Vinnie. Vinnie and my father kept the name because it was a very popular place in Revere. Unfortunately after he made a few bucks from it he decided to improve the place. He spent money revamping the shop and changed it into a combination doughnut store and ice cream parlor. As soon as he finished the business went out the window.

You can say one thing for my father: he was willing to try anything. He got knocked down a lot of times, but he always bounced

"Having [my parents] behind me has been the most important thing in my life."

"The course that I followed all through baseball was started right there [on the Sparks]." Conigliaro is center, middle row.

After signing with the Red Sox (left to right: brother Billy, mother, TC, Red Sox scout Milt Bolling). (Photo courtesy of UPI)

After homering in first Fenway Park at-bat: "When I got back to the dugout they were all standing up and clapping." (Photo courtesy of Jerry Buckley)

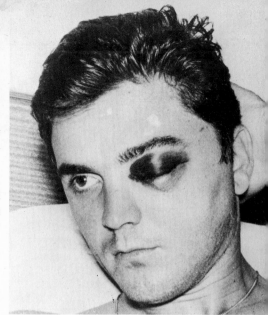

"What I saw . . . sickened me. The left eye was all black and purple and was about the size of a handball." (Photo courtesy of UPI)

"The fact [that fans] wanted to communicate with me when I was down made me feel even better than I did in the good times." (Photo courtesy of Wide World)

"I [said] I'd be back in the big leagues . . . next year, pitching."
(Photo courtesy of Wide World)

"I had never felt so low and beaten in my whole life. I had just struck out for the eighth time in my last 10 at-bats."
(Photo courtesy of UPI)

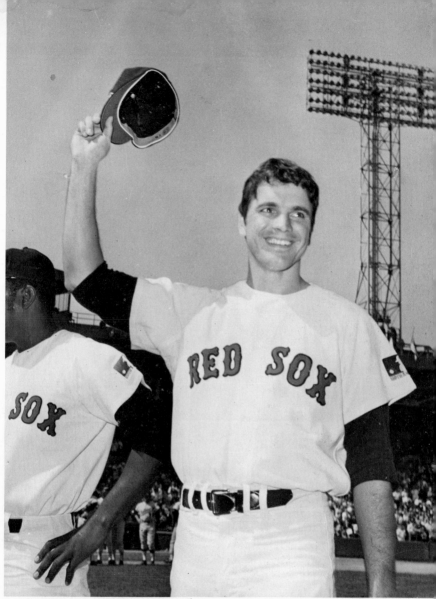

Return to Fenway Park: "I was grinning and shivering at the same time. I stood there . . . and listened to the beautiful sound coming from all those people." (Photo courtesy of UPI)

"I suddenly had a feeling come over me. . . . *I survived. I made my comeback. . . . I've made it.* . . . And that's when I started smacking the ball." (Photo courtesy of *Sports Illustrated*)

back. He's never quit anything in his life. When he was single he used to shovel horse manure at the Boston Rodeo for $1 a day; then he'd deliver the manure to Caruso's Farm in East Boston and spread it around—all for the same dollar.

When I was one year old he went into the chicken business. He brought home some fifty young chicks and built a shack out in the back where he could incubate them. He kept adding chicks all the time and eventually he raised as many as 500 chickens. This was just after the war and chickens were hard to come by because the government had appropriated a lot of them. So they were expensive, and my father figured the fatter the chickens got the more he'd make from them. People would come to the house begging for chickens but he said oh no, he was going to hold off till they were nice and fat. Chickens were selling for sixty-five to seventy cents a pound then, and he figured when the time came he was going to make a real killing.

Now in those days my father was making $60 a week at the zipper factory and spending $35 of it feeding the chickens; we lived on the balance. He had a mortgage on the house and was in the process of remodeling it, and he was still running the doughnut shop. At times the money was so low that once, when he decided to buy slipcovers for our furniture, he paid the guy off in chickens. But he still wouldn't sell any. When we were hungry my mother would go down in the cellar with one of the chickens and slaughter it for supper.

All of a sudden the government freed the chicken market and the price dropped to about twenty-six cents a pound. My father decided to keep the hens and sell the eggs, but the hens came down with chicken pox and began dying off at the rate of about twenty a day. When it was all over, all he had left was $60, and as he still likes to say, "a chicken coop filled with chicken shit." At this time my father had a moustache and he immediately became known in the neighborhood as the villain of the chicken yard.

Eventually, he joined the Triangle Tool and Dye Company, in Lynn, Massachusetts, and he's worked there for the past fourteen years. He's a plant manager there today. Charley Feingold, the president and owner of the company, has been one of my father's closest friends ever since. During the years my father continues to try new businesses on the side, and every time they fail Charley is there to bail him out. My father's been trying to cool it, but we never know when he's going to try again.

The only friend I remember having at this time was a kid named Frisky. He lived right next door to us. He became the first guy I ever tried to beat at anything. He was two years older than I was. We used to race all the time and he always beat me. It was hard for me to accept. No matter how many times he beat me I still thought I'd win the next time. I don't know where he is today, but I wish I did because I sure would like to race him again.

Before I was old enough to go to school, I'd get up every day, put on my sneakers, ask my mother to tie the laces for me and run out the front door to the ballfield across the street from my house. I'd stay there all day, till my mother had to come down and drag me home for supper at night. That's all I wanted to do. I was there so much that the other mothers in the neighborhood began saying my mother wasn't a very good one because she let me stay out there all the time. On top of that I was so skinny that it looked like my mother was starving me.

I stayed in the park so much that my mother finally decided to enroll me in a private kindergarten, just to keep the other mothers from having something to talk about. I didn't care for kindergarten. I didn't like being cooped up all the time. My mind was always someplace else. So, I once cut kindergarten for a whole week. I'd leave the house pretending I was going around the corner where a station wagon picked us up. But I'd hide instead, and as soon as the wagon left I'd sneak back the other way across our backyard and hide in the shack my father had built. I'd spend the rest of the time there till I figured the station wagon was due back. Then I'd sneak back out there and come back the front way as though I'd been to school.

My mother finally found out about it when she went down to the school one day and asked a teacher how Anthony was doing. The teacher said how should she know, she hadn't seen Anthony in a week. That's when I received my first beating. My mother chased me around the house with a wooden spoon she used to stir spaghetti. She chased me up the stairs into her bedroom. I made a head-first slide under the bed, just out of her reach. I thought I was safe. She kept on saying, "Come on out of there, come on out." Then she grabbed my foot with one hand and pulled me out, while whacking me with the spoon. She hit me so hard the spoon broke in half. Now all I had to look forward to was my father coming home from work and hearing all about it.

Just before he got home that night, I sneaked downstairs and hid in the cellar. When I heard him come in I listened through the door. My mother told him what I'd done. I heard my father say in a loud voice, "Where is he? Where is that kid? I'm gonna break him in half." My father had a tremendous temper in those days. When he came down to look for me in the cellar I hid behind the boiler. I must have been down there for about three hours when I realized how hungry I was. Finally, when I couldn't stand it, I sneaked upstairs and tiptoed up to the refrigerator and got out some food. But my mother heard me go in, she grabbed me and said, "Your father wants to talk to you."

I started crying. "Oh, no," I said, "he's gonna beat me up. He's not gonna talk to me." She dragged me into the living room where my father was sitting. I was frightened to death. But he didn't put a hand on me this time. All he did was give me my first serious warning in life. "If you ever skip school again," he told me, "I'm really going to let you have it." Then he sent me to my room. I was relieved, but I realized then that if I ever stepped out of line I'd always have to answer to my father.

When I was in the second grade my teacher didn't like me. I was a little wise guy, I'm sure, and she made me stay after class almost every day. One day she asked me for my homework, and I hadn't done it. She put me in a closet. When she let the class out later I was still in the closet. She had forgot about me. I didn't hear anything and I tried to get out. But the door was locked. I got scared. I began yelling for someone to come and get me, but nobody came. I began crying. I don't know how much longer I stayed in there, but finally my mother and father showed up. They had tracked me down. When they let me out of that closet I was the happiest little kid in the world. A week later they took me out of that school and enrolled me in a private school.

It didn't matter. I never got along too well in school, either with my teachers or my classmates. I was apart from the other kids for some reason. I think I was stupid; I wasn't as quick as the other kids; I was very slow and I lacked concentration. It took me longer than anyone else to learn how to read and write. A lot of the kids made fun of me, so I stayed by myself mostly. As a result I'd skip school quite a bit, in spite of my father's warning, and I accepted the beatings.

The worst beating I ever got happened some years later. When I was eight we moved out of Revere to East Boston, which was only about five miles away. My dad was doing better at the zipper factory and he bought a nice little house on Crestway Road for about $10,000 or $12,000. It was in a quiet neighborhood just behind Suffolk Downs. One day my mother asked me to go to the store for her. For some reason I was in a pretty rotten mood and said, "No, I'm not going." So she then asked my brother Billy, who is a couple of years younger than I am. He looked up to me and because I wasn't going he said he wouldn't go, too. So she asked little Richie but Richie was big enough to see how things worked, so he said no, too. Now my mother began crying. We had been nagging her all day and she was at the end of her rope. She called up my father and told him what had happened. He left work in the middle of the day and came home. "Come here," he said to me, "I want to talk to you, Choo." (My father has always called me Choo, because I crawled so fast as a baby I reminded him of a choo-choo train.)

Well, I thought he really wanted to talk to me this time, and I went with him. And he said to me, "So, you think you're a big man, huh? Telling your mother you're not going to the store for her." And I said no, I didn't think I was such a big man, and he said, "Well, I'm going to teach you something right now." He began whacking me with his hands all over the house. I was crying, my mother was crying, and I could hear my two brothers who were hiding upstairs crying. He kept banging me around and everybody was screaming. Then he dragged me downstairs to the cellar, took off his belt and started hitting me with it. After he was through with me, he went looking for Billy and Richie. He found Billy hiding under the bed and Richie in my mother's closet. He gave both of them a beating. Afterwards, the three of us, still whimpering from the licking my father had given us, walked down the street together to the store to buy my mother whatever it was she wanted.

I remember the next day I hated my father's guts. I didn't want to see him again and I got ready to run away from home. I got an old pillowcase from my mother's closet and packed a few of my things in it. I also left room for my ball, bat and glove. I got about halfway up the hill from my house and I hid under a tree. I fell asleep for a couple of hours and when I woke up I decided I didn't want to run away anymore because my mother's cooking was so good. So I went back to the house; nobody seemed to have missed me. But I like to think back to that time as a sort of turning point in my life. I think I stopped being such a wise guy after that, at least to my mother. That was the last beating my father ever gave me. We still talk about it today and can laugh about it now. But at the time I really hated my father for it.

We were a close family, but with three boys around the house in an Italian family there was always a lot of screaming and hollering, and, of course, we had our share of fights. Mostly, between Billy and Richie. As the older brother I always felt sort of superior to my brothers. It's not that I felt I could do anything better than they could. It's just as the oldest I felt I was the man in charge. They both looked up to me—they still do today. We used to fight among ourselves, but if anybody else started up with one of us they wound up fighting the whole Conigliaro family.

Once I remember my brother Richie was playing outside with some little kids from next door. Richie and another kid got into a little scuffle and started throwing fists. I was looking out the window and when I saw the fight start I called Billy over, "Hey, look at Richie go." We could see Richie was doing a pretty good job on the other guy and we were laughing and cheering him on. Of course, my brother Richie didn't know we were watching, but we were happy to see him winning the fight.

While we were watching, the other kid's big sister came out of their house and tried to break it up. When she couldn't, she picked up a plastic machine gun they had been playing with and busted it over Richie's head. The gun broke into a hundred pieces and my brother fell over and was lying on the ground without moving. I went out that door like a shot, but by the time I got there she had taken her brother into the house. I went up and rang their doorbell. She came to the door and started to say, "Well, what do you want?" but the words never got all the way out because I smacked her right in the mouth and knocked her down. Then I went back and picked up my brother and took him back inside our house. Richie had a pretty good lump on his head and he was groggy. When my mother asked me what happened I told her. Then the mother of the other two kids came over and she started yelling at my mother and calling her all kinds of names, and my mother began yelling back at her, and I thought I was going to see another fist fight break out. My mother really stood up for me; she didn't blame me for hitting that girl. We didn't get along with that family too well for a long time, until we all got older.

That was one of the two times I ever attempted to hit a girl. The other time came years later when I was a senior in St. Mary's High School in Lynn, and I almost hit a nun. She was my teacher, and for some reason she hated me. She seemed to take delight in being especially mean to me. She would tell me to stand up in class and say to me in front of everyone else, "So, Mr. Conigliaro, you want to be a ballplayer, do you? Well, you'll never make it because you're no good," and she'd keep me after school when I wanted to get out to the ballpark.

I remember once in my sophomore year I really worked hard on a science project on how the heart works. I had a cow's heart and I dissected it, explaining the intricacies of blood flow. I thought I had done an excellent job, but when it was finished she gave me a C, which was just barely passing.

It got worse: she actually called me names no nun ever should use. She called me "wop," and "guinea," and would tell me off in front of the whole class. She really drove me insane, and I remember whenever my mother came up to ask her what was the matter she'd go into an act and say, "Oh, Mrs. Conigliaro, isn't it nice to see you again." So she made it difficult for my mother to deal with the situation.

In my senior year I had her again and she picked up right where she'd left off. She said I didn't have enough guts to become a professional athlete. One time I remember I had a badly sprained ankle from a football injury. I came to class with crutches, and she called me a phony, saying there was nothing really wrong with my ankle. I had had enough, and one day decided to get even with her. I got two of my friends whom she had also been needling in class and said, "Look, tomorrow, in class, let's beat her up. When she's sitting up front while we're doing our assignment, let's sneak up to her desk and really give it to her." I could see they were just as excited about it as I was, and they agreed to come along with me.

Next day, while we were supposed to be writing something at our desks, I gave them the signal and we started moving up to the front, all of us walking in a low crouch. I was in the front. I turned around and saw them behind me and signaled us forward. As I got about two steps from her, I turned around to give another signal and noticed they weren't there: both of them had run back to their seats. She suddenly looked up, and saw me in a low, menacing crouch ready to pounce on her. "Well, Mr. Conigliaro," she said, "what do you want?" I didn't have any answer.

As I said earlier, playing baseball was something I liked to do when I was very young. My father didn't try to get me interested in it because he thought I'd be good at it and become a major-leaguer. But I think we both began to get that idea after my first Little League tryout when I was eight years old. We had just moved to East Boston. One day my Uncle Vinnie, who was president of the Little League in Revere, told me next time I was near the Little League field I should go up and see Mr. Ben Campbell, who coached the team in East Boston. He was the coach of the Orient Park Sparks in East Boston. One day I saw him working with the team. I went up to him and said, "Are you Mr. Campbell?" When he said he was I told him, "I'm Tony Conigliaro. My uncle, Vinnie Martelli, told me to stop by and say hello. I want to play in the Little League."

I was still pretty small and skinny. He looked down at me and said, "How old are you, Tony? You look very young."

"I'm eight," I answered.

"Well, you have to be nine to play in the Little League," he said. "But your uncle told me about you. Do you want to work out with us now?"

I said sure, and he told me to go out in the field and pick up some grounders. Right away I noticed that all the other kids were older and bigger than I was. But it didn't bother me because I could tell I was probably as good as any of them and maybe even better. Mr. Campbell saw that, too, because after about five minutes he came up to me and said, "Yes, I think you can play ball. You can't be on the team till next year, but if you want to work out with us you're welcome. Then when you're nine we can make it official."

I couldn't say yes fast enough. After that, whenever I worked out with the team I could see the other kids were amazed at how hard I hit the ball. Frankly, I was amazed, too.

My father kept encouraging me to play baseball. When I wasn't working out with the Little League team I worked out with my brother Billy. On hot Saturday afternoons when most of the other kids my age were down on the beach sunning themselves, I was down at Ambro's Park in the Orient Heights section of East Boston. We had two baseballs, all taped up because they were so worn out, and a grubby old bat. We'd play a game. Billy would throw me the two baseballs and I'd hit them. I'd hit them as far as I could, go get them, come back, then I'd pitch the two balls at him. He'd hit them as far as he could, go get them, come back, then throw to me again. We'd do this back and forth all day long.

During these years my Uncle Vinnie was always there to help me. I always have felt that anything I became in baseball I owe to my Uncle Vinnie because of all the time he spent with me when I was a kid. He used to pitch batting practice to me for hours, till my hands bled. I developed calluses on my hands at ten, and I remember that nothing would make me stop. Not the calluses, or the bleeding, or anything. I just kept hitting. For some reason I got a big charge out of hitting a baseball a long way, a real big thrill. And I kept on swinging. Yes, it gave me a sort of sense of power. I felt that I was working at something I really loved, and I could see progress. I could see myself becoming a better ballplayer than anybody else.

I finally got to be nine years old and I joined the Sparks and got my own uniform. This must have been what I was always waiting for, because it felt natural putting it on. I was still pretty small and skinny, but Mr. Campbell liked the way I moved and told me he was going to put me on second base. "I don't think you throw hard enough yet to play shortstop," he said. I couldn't have cared less. I just wanted to play, and where I played didn't matter. I also wanted to hit, and I batted either third or fourth most of that season. That told me something. Here I was, the youngest kid on the team, and he was using me in the power slots. In my very first at-bat for the Sparks I hit a home run over the center-field fence.

I still felt very strange around the team. For one thing, my family had only just moved to East Boston, and for another, I never had any close friends before. Now I was in a strange town playing on a Little League team and I was making close friends for the first time in my life: all of a sudden I wasn't a loner anymore. I think Ben Campbell had a lot to do with this. He was a very kind man and I remember thinking of him then as my second father. He was very patient with everybody. He liked my swing and told me not to change it for anybody. Whenever I was in the batting cage I could see the other kids watching me closely. They admired the way I hit that damn baseball and I liked knowing they watched me. I wasn't that stupid kid in school anymore.

By the time I turned ten, I had begun to shoot up; I also grew stronger and Mr. Campbell moved me to shortstop and made me his cleanup hitter. One day he was hitting us grounders in fielding practice and the ball took a bad hop and nearly skulled me. I flinched. Later he came over to me holding a baseball in his hand. "Tony," he said, "if you're afraid of this little baseball, then forget it. Maybe you shouldn't be a ballplayer." I told him no, nothing was going to make me quit, and that I'd never do it again. And I didn't.

I knew he liked me and I did almost everything Mr. Campbell asked me to do. One time I disobeyed him. We were playing a game one day and we had two runners in scoring position. I looked down to him for a sign and he gave me the take sign. When the pitch came in it was a beauty, so I decided to hit it anyway. I got a hit and knocked in both runs. But after the game he came up to me and said, "You're on the bench next game, Tony." I asked him why, but I knew.

I played shortstop and pitched during my remaining three years with the Sparks. I was probably the only guy in the league who threw a legitimate curve ball that broke. I think the best game I played in those years was the day I pitched a no-hitter and a kid called Brother Florintine pitched a one-hitter. We won the game. During those years it was baseball day and night. I wanted to be the best. I never tried to pattern myself after anybody. I hardly knew anything about big-league ballplayers. In fact, I hardly ever went to Fenway Park to see the Red Sox play. If I had a choice between watching a game and playing in one, I always played. I think I saw Ted Williams play only once.

All I wanted to do was improve and be the best. One day after a game I went over to Mr. Campbell and asked him if he'd mind hitting me a few balls in the outfield. He said, "Anytime you want, Tony." That's the kind of great man he was. He loved baseball as much as I did. He didn't get out of work till around four o'clock; then he'd head over for the ballfield and we'd play a game. After that he'd hit me some balls in the outfield. Even though I was a shortstop, I felt I needed experience out there. It got to be a daily ritual. My folks would come out there and so would Mrs. Campbell, and as soon as the game was over they'd find seats somewhere and he'd hit to me until it was too dark to see the ball. Every kid in the world should have a Little League coach like Mr. Campbell. He worked with me, taught me the correct way to do things, the real fundamentals. It's so important for a kid to get started on the right foot. I think that the course that I followed all through baseball was started right there under Mr. Campbell.

Soon I discovered how much I hated to lose. There were a couple of times we lost the final game which could have meant a state championship. I remember I used to cry, the manager used to cry, and everybody on our ballclub used to cry. I don't cry anymore when we lose a ballgame, but I'm still pretty upset. And I learned that there's only one way to play. That's to go out and give 100 percent and try to do all you can to win a ballgame.

I was probably the best hitter on the team during those four years. I don't exactly remember all my averages but they were always better than .400. I worked at hitting: I just didn't hit the ball and feel good about it. I would ask myself why I hit the ball well, or why I didn't. I worked on my balance. I was always checking to see where my feet and hands were. Looking back on it now, I realize how lucky I really was. What a lot of people don't realize is that many kids reach their peak as players when they're still at the Little League age and they never really get much better. That's why you see some promising kids never make it when they get older. The question with me then was whether I was reaching my full potential or would I continue to improve.

After I got out of Little League I went right into the Pony League. I was now thirteen years old. One thing I'll never forget was the time we went to Newburgh, New York, to play in an eastern division elimination tournament. We were a club mostly of cocky Italians and some people didn't like us. The man who made all the arrangements for the teams put all the teams but ours in air-conditioned rooms at the hotel, but when we got there he said they didn't have any air-conditioned rooms left. This was in the late summer. One day I was walking on the field, I looked out toward the fence in left and I said to this same man, "Hey, how far out is that fence?"

He said, "It's 340, but don't worry, none of your guys is going to reach it."

I said, "Oh, yeah, well I betcha I can hit three out of ten over that fence right now," and I asked one of our pitchers named Muzzy, who's real name was Bobby Mazzarino, to pitch to me. I hit four of them out, and I mean way out. The man just stood there looking stunned and then he walked away.

We came close to winning the whole thing. We won our first two games, and were leading 5–3 in the third game. Then Brother Florintine misjudged a fly ball to make it 5–4. The next guy hit a grounder to me at short, and the first-baseman couldn't handle my low throw and the tying run came in from third. At this point I was brought in to pitch. I pitched five scoreless innings and we finally won the game. Because I had worked those five innings I couldn't start the final against Levittown and we lost. I've always felt that if I could have pitched that last game we would have won.

While baseball was my favorite sport I played any game you care to mention. I always had to be the best. When I was about ten years old, I received a pair of ice skates for Christmas. I didn't know how to skate then, but I wanted to learn. So I would get the skates, take some fruit with me, and go down over by the race track. I'd climb a barbed wire fence to get to a spot where there was a frozen-over oil slick. I was embarrassed at not knowing how to skate. So I spent hours trying to teach myself. I went down there because I knew no one would see me making a fool of myself, falling, getting up, falling back down again. I actually learned how to skate backwards before I learned to skate frontwards.

When I thought I was ready to be seen by the public, I headed for Ambro's Park, where I'd played so much baseball. In the winters they used to flood the field so the kids could skate on it. I minded my own business and watched a hockey game and then realized that I could skate better than the other kids my age. So I bought a Northern Pro hockey stick, and got into games with the older kids.

' My father never seemed too interested in what I had to say about my hockey accomplishments when I got home. Every time I mentioned some shot I had made, he changed the subject. All he'd ever say was, "Be careful, it's a dangerous sport." When I was fourteen and ready to go into high school, my dad told me how he really felt about my playing hockey. He said he thought I had a good future in baseball and that I ought to concentrate on that. He said, "I'm not going to force you to do anything. Sure, you're a hell of a skater, but I think you're a better ball-player. If you play hockey in high school you'll take a chance of ruining your opportunities."

I didn't like it, but he had been right so far. So I agreed to give up hockey, and in the next breath I asked him for a basketball hoop and a backboard that I could put up in the backyard. He said all right, so it started all over again. I hadn't spent much time on basketball, but now I wanted to be the best at it. I dribbled and shot all day long. Mostly, I concentrated on shooting. Again, I did it by myself because I knew I'd be embarrassed if anybody knew I couldn't do something well. I used to play basketball in the snow, on the ice—it didn't matter. My brother Billy and I rigged up a light on the back porch so we could play at night. This was only four months before I went to high school.

By the time I got into St. Mary's, I was good enough to make the freshman team. I couldn't dribble very well but I had a helluva shot. In my first basketball game we were playing Eastern Junior High School. I'd never really played with a team before; I had just shot baskets in my backyard. I tried to learn the game, but we only had two weeks of practice before our opener. I was playing forward. The ball was tapped to me, I took a half-court set shot, and *swish*, the ball went right in the basket. I heard cheerleaders giving me a cheer, yelling out, "Hey Tony, Hey C."

Suddenly, I remembered that our school didn't have any cheerleaders and I wondered why the heck they were cheering me. Then I found out that I had shot at the wrong basket. We lost that ballgame by one point. It took me a while, but I finally managed to live that boner down. Instead of giving up, I worked harder, and in my senior year I set a new St. Mary's scoring record with 417 points.

Around the neighborhood we also used to play a game called tag rush, which is like touch football in most other parts of the country. We played it on our block on Crestway Road, right in front of our house. I always played quarterback—tailback, really—because I had a good arm. One day after I had finished playing I was staring out the window watching my younger brother Richie playing catch with one of his friends. The street we lived on was completely downhill, and the football got away and began rolling down the hill. A car was coming up the street and ran over the ball, busting it. It looked to me like the driver had deliberately run over the football. Richie ran over and started hollering at the guy, and he got out of the car and pushed Richie, knocking him down.

In about one-eighth of a second I was out of the house and down the steps after the guy, who must have been about fifty years old. When I got there he had just got back inside the car and closed the door. I opened it, jumped in and started choking him and biting him. I almost went insane. The guy was screaming, "Leave me alone. Leave me alone." Finally, I caught hold of myself and ran back to the house. My brother Billy tells me, looking back on it, that he thought I was crazy. Maybe I was, but I have never been able to stand it when anybody puts a hand on either of my brothers.

By the time I was ready to enter high school, I had built up a pretty good reputation in the area as an athlete. Lenny Merullo, who had been a major-league ballplayer back during the war, had seen me play a lot and recommended me to St. John's Prep, which was in Danvers, about fifteen miles out of East Boston. My father got a call from a Brother Gilroy and went down to see him.

My father also went to talk to the people at St. Mary's, which was a little closer in Lynn. In fact, the school was just around the corner from the Triangle Tool and Dye Company, where my father worked. Nipper Clancy was the baseball coach and my father was also friendly with people like Father Johnson and Sister Henora. He finally decided that would be the best place for me to go. He could drive me to school in the morning and take me home at night.

Just about the time he decided, the people at St. John's got in touch and offered me a scholarship, which would have amounted to about $2,000 a year. Now my father wasn't exactly the wealthiest guy in the world and it was a tempting offer. But he stuck with his decision for me to go to St. Mary's. It also offered me a scholarship, but it was very small and my father said give it to some kid who might need it more than I did. Unfortunately, after my freshman year at St. Mary's, Nipper Clancy retired and both Father Johnson and Sister Henora were transferred to another school. Now all our friends were gone and I was at the mercy of a school that never really accepted me. It was now that I got into all that difficulty with my teacher. About the only thing that really saved me was the fact that I starred in baseball, basketball, and football and was fortunate to be named Most Valuable Player in all three sports by the time I graduated.

Besides, I never really cared for school. I just couldn't stand being cooped up. My mind was always off in the wild blue yonder. I just didn't care about history and Napoleon and Latin. In my senior year there were several big colleges interested in me because of my sports, and I considered going to college. But not very seriously: I knew I wanted to play baseball more than anything else.

It's a good thing I was so interested in sports—or else I don't know how I would have wound up. When I wasn't playing ball, I was getting in trouble. I did nothing really serious, just mischievous things like throwing snowballs at passing cars with my brother Billy, or harassing the people across the street because we were sure they lived in a haunted house. I didn't know what to do with myself when there wasn't a game. I saw a girl one day across from my house walking in the snow and I ran to my closet and got my BB-gun; then I went to the window and just as she bent over I fired and hit her right in the seat of her pants. That's the kind of thing I did, and when I was caught my parents made me stay in at night for a couple of weeks.

Once I took a job as a shoeshine boy just to keep busy, but this lasted only about three days when all I made was about fifty cents. With Suffolk Downs right behind my house, I decided one day to make some real money. I went over to the track and waited for the people to come out early. I asked them to give me their programs, which they paid twenty-five cents for inside. Then I sold them for ten cents apiece to the people arriving late. On good days I made about $3. Then I'd go off and buy myself some candy.

I think I must have been around fifteen years old when I discovered what girls were all about. Oh, it's not as though I didn't notice them until I was fifteen; in fact, I have always been impressed by girls and I'd go crazy on the beach figuring out ways of how to touch them without them getting sore at me. Later on, I learned that some of them liked to be touched, but until I found that out I lived with this beautiful terror inside me.

Even though I lived in a nice neighborhood, it was still tough. There were a lot of fights, sometimes even gang fights. I had my share of them, partly because I really wasn't too popular around the Lynn area when I attended St. Mary's. I was getting a lot of publicity because of sports, and I remember what a friend of mine once told me when I was in Little League. He said, "Jealousy destroys all reason," and that statement has always stuck with me. So I think that was one of the main reasons why I had so much trouble in high school.

In my senior year our last football game was scheduled against a combined team from three high schools in Lynn. They had been needling us, calling us pansies. Before that game I was at a St. Mary's High School dance, and I had driven there in my father's 1959 Cadillac. I remember a cop came in asking for me and told me that somebody had smashed in all the windows of my father's car. I went outside and I saw they had all been broken in with bricks. There were a couple of tough guys out there and

139

I recognized them as members of the Lynn team we were going to play. I could see they wanted to fight me and I went crazy. I said, "Fine, let's go, right now." But they backed off and said, "No, not here, meet us down at Lynn Beach." Now I knew what that meant: Lynn Beach is where they all hung out and if I went I knew I was sure to get stomped on. I wasn't about to get a gang of mine together, go down there and start a riot. So I cooled it somehow, and the incident passed by with no fists flying.

A night or two later I was in Roland's Ice Cream Parlor in Lynn with a friend of mine, Mike Cavanaugh. When we left Mike got in his car and drove away and I headed for mine. But all of a sudden another car drove up behind mine so that I couldn't get out. I jumped out of the car and saw these guys coming for me, two colored guys and four white guys, from the same pack who played for Lynn. I remembered that I had a hammer in the car because I had just repaired the backboard in our yard; I jumped in and grabbed the hammer. Then I jumped out of the car, backed up against the wall waving the hammer in their faces and started swearing at them. "All right," I yelled, "just stay away from me or so help me the first guy that gets close is going to get this right in the head."

Luckily, they backed off and got back in their car. I got back in mine and headed for home. But I noticed they were following me. My six-cylinder Chevy couldn't go very fast and I saw they were gaining on me. I realized they were going to try and run me off the road. *They were trying to kill me,* I told myself. I was terrified. I stepped down as far as I could on the accelerator and somehow managed to get home all right. I jumped out of the car and ran inside the house and woke up my father. We got a couple of bats and went to the front of the house. If they decided to pull up and start trouble, we were going to charge them. But they didn't do a thing.

The incident, of course, upset my whole family, and this was one time I was glad I asked for help. Later on we reported the whole thing to the cops and they told us they knew the kids and that some of them had records. I was still mad and wanted revenge.

I got it in the game. We beat them 22–6, and I think one of the reasons we won by that margin was that I was so keyed-up. But we really rocked and socked it to them that day, running up our twenty-two points in the first half. But in the third quarter I became a little lackadaisical. Our coach liked tricky formations, such as unbalanced lines, and he taught us some of the new stuff for this game.

I was the quarterback and in the third quarter I called a play with an unbalanced line. The signal was supposed to be on two. As we got up to the line of scrimmage, I put my hands down and began the count. "Team ready, set. Hut one, hut two . . . hut three, hut four . . ." The ball never came back and I thought my center, Jimmy Driscoll, must have missed the number. So I shouted, "Will you give me the goddamn ball!"; but as I looked down I saw I was standing behind our right tackle. Jimmy Driscoll was two men over to the right still hanging onto the ball. He started laughing so hard he fell down and we got a delay of game penalty of five yards. I'm glad we won that game for several reasons, but especially because the win gave St. Mary's its best record in history.

As I've said, thank God for sports. They took up so much of my time in St. Mary's I didn't get into all the trouble I might have otherwise. My father drove me to school every morning; afterwards, he'd come over and watch practice—it could be baseball, basketball, or football—and when it was over he'd drive me home. We'd normally get back to the house around seven o'clock every night.

As usual, my father was right: baseball was my best sport and I was scouted for most of my four years at St. Mary's. It began when I was still a sophomore, but that was really by accident. We were scheduled to play a game against St. John's and I was going to pitch against a kid named Danny Murphy. He was a senior and was then regarded as one of the hottest baseball products in the entire New England area. So the scouts came out that day in droves, because once the season was over they'd be coming at him with all kinds of big money offers. Danny gave up only four hits that day, but I got three of them. Later on I read in the papers that the Cubs had signed him for $100,000. I was only a sophomore in high school at the time, but I had my dreams, too. $100,000. Wow, I thought to myself, if that could only be me.

As a result of that game, the scouts became a little more aware of me. I know that Al Lopez, who was then managing the Chicago White Sox, was there, and Nipper Clancy sat with him and told him to keep an eye on me. The Red Sox had a scout named Milt Bolling, who had played shortstop for them back in the 1950's, and he started coming out regularly. I'm hardly exaggerating when I say there were games when there were more scouts in the stands than spectators. They were all over the place. Some of them liked to sit around the home plate area to watch me hit. Others sat together and checked notes with one another. Others liked to walk down the baseline a bit and watch me in the field. Afterwards, some of them would walk over and tell me how much I was going to like Detroit or Cincinnati or Baltimore. Sometimes, one of the scouts would take my family and me out to dinner, all in the interest of softening us up when the time came to talk. All together, I knew by my senior year that there were about fourteen teams really interested in signing me. I felt the pressure, sure, but it was a nice kind of pressure, the kind that made me play all the harder.

In my junior and senior years, I hit over .600 and won about sixteen ballgames as a pitcher. In games I didn't pitch I played either third base or shortstop. When I was a senior, Billy entered St. Mary's, and made the team, too. He didn't play much that year because he broke an arm, but there was one game that I remember because we collaborated on the win. We played a very tough game against a team called Matignon, and I pitched. I gave up five hits and struck out ten hitters. We won, 3–2, and Billy singled in the fifth to give us a 2–1 lead, then knocked in the winning run in the seventh with a double. With my 3 hits, the Conigliaro brothers collected exactly half of the hits our club got in that game. It was an especially satisfying season for me because St. Mary's won its first Catholic Conference Championship that year.

When the high school season ended, I decided to play American Legion ball that summer. I had been playing for the Connery Post No. 6 team the past couple of summers and I felt I owed the team one more season. That meant I couldn't negotiate or sign with a major-league team until the Legion season ended in early September. Since I was also a .600 hitter in Legion ball, I felt one more good season wouldn't hurt my chances of getting a good contract when the scouts came around.

One day, while the Legion season was still on, the Red Sox phoned me and asked me to come to Fenway Park for a special workout. I knew what that meant, since I had gone through it once before. They would have their top scouts on hand to watch and that would help them decide just how much they really wanted you. When I got there, I found they had also invited another player. He was a young man from California, also seventeen years old, named Tony Horton. He had flown in all the way from California for this special workout, and I realized that the Red Sox were still undecided as to whom they were going to give their big bonus money.

Neil Mahoney, the Red Sox chief scout, came up to us and told us how the workout would go. "Horton, you pitch to Conigliaro for a while," he said, "then switch." I was still a very thin kid. I was seventeen and I stood at six feet three inches and weighed about 170 pounds. I couldn't hit the ball very far then, but I could run fast and I had a good arm. Tony Horton pitched to me and I began hitting line drives all over the ballpark. I thought I was doing pretty good, and I felt they were impressed, too.

Next it was my turn to pitch to Horton. He then weighed around 210 pounds and you could see his muscles bulging out in all the right places. He came up and hit the first pitch I threw him into the center-field bleachers. The next pitch I threw him went into the Red Sox bullpen. He hit a couple more into the screen in left field. Suddenly, I heard Mahoney yell down to us, "Okay, that's enough. We've seen enough."

Enough? I hadn't even worked up a sweat yet. But that was the end of it. I went down to the locker room, showered and dressed, and went home. Mahoney said we'd be hearing from him when the American Legion season was over. But sometime just before our last game I read in the Boston papers that the Red Sox had signed Tony Horton for $125,000. My heart sank, but in the next second I told myself, if they're giving away that kind of money I can probably do as well.

My father had written letters to all the clubs interested in me

144

that I would be eligible to talk contract on September 10, and a whole string of appointments was set up for that day. Starting at nine o'clock in the morning they came one right after another, all day long, till seven or eight that night. My father and I had a pretty good idea about which teams were really serious, and we also thought we knew how much money we were going to get. Tony Horton had signed for $125,000, Danny Murphy had gone for $100,000, and some other local kids like Billy Madden and Bobby Guindon had gone for the same amount. Just before the first scout came into the house, my father said to me, "Well Choo, we're really going to do it today."

The first guy came in, sat down, and said to my father, "Mr. Conigliaro, we'd like to offer your son $8,000." When I heard that I nearly dropped dead. I couldn't believe my ears. Maybe he'd said $80,000, I thought. No, he really had said $8,000. My father could see the disappointment in my face, and after the guy left he turned to me and said, "Don't worry, Choo. All the other clubs still have to come in. By the time we get to the end of the day, we should be doing pretty well." You know, my father the businessman.

But as the other clubs marched in and out the money didn't get too much better. After a while we came to the sad realization that we weren't going to come up with the big money we were expecting. They all tried to explain to us that the new rules change that year made it difficult for the clubs to throw around as much money as they had in past years, and that most of them were just going for one big hot prospect and then they'd scale the other bonuses down pretty sharply.

The Red Sox were the next-to-last club to visit us. Neil Mahoney and Milt Bolling came in, and the best offer they made us came to $20,000 with some fringe benefits. I had been hoping to sign with the Red Sox for several reasons: it meant I'd get a chance to play in my home town; there was that great left-field wall at Fenway Park that was built for right-hand pull hitters; and the Red Sox didn't have an overload of good outfielders. They had young Carl Yastrzemski, but after him fellows like Lou Clinton, Gary Geiger and Roman Mejias. I figured I could crack that outfield in a couple of seasons.

That was another factor, I believe, in the amount of money they offered me. They knew, and I realized, that I was far from ready to play in the majors. I'd have to go out for seasoning, while they figured Tony Horton was a lot readier than I was. My father listened and bargained and told them the same thing he told all the others—we'll let you know later on in the day.

The Orioles were the last team we spoke to. They offered us exactly the same deal as the Red Sox did. My father told them, "For another $5,000 you can have him." The scout said he'd have to call Bill DeWitt back in Baltimore for permission, so we told him to go ahead and make the call. He did, but I guess DeWitt said no, because he didn't change his offer. So he left, and then we sat around talking it over and decided it might as well be the Red Sox. We called them up and around ten o'clock that night Mahoney and Bolling were back at the house and I signed a contract with the Red Sox.

Looking back on it now, it became a pretty happy scene even if we fell far short of our money expectations. After signing and posing for pictures with me wearing a Red Sox cap, my parents opened up a bottle of chilled champagne and we had a little celebration. My Uncle Vinnie, who really had done so much to make all this possible, was there, just beaming. Also Joe Tauro, who recently had become our lawyer, came over to have a look at the contract; and of course, Billy and Richie were as happy as if it had just happened to them.

At one point, Neil Mahoney said to my father, "You know, your boy is a pretty good ballplayer. But he has no power."

"Come on, now," my father said. "He sure does have power."

And Mahoney said, "Well, what can you say? He's your boy, after all."

"That's not so," my father said. "His name's on that paper now. He's all yours. Why should I say it now?"

After everybody went home, my father and I were sitting alone too tired to get up and go to bed, and suddenly, out of all that exhaustion and thinking back on all the years we had been working toward this one goal, the two of us burst into hysterical laughter. We were completely out of control. My father lifted his glass with what was the last of the champagne and he said, "Well, Choo, how does it feel to be a millionaire?"

In October the Red Sox sent me to Bradenton for the Winter Instructional League. This is a good way for ballclubs to give their young kids additional work and to have a better idea by spring training of what they can do. It was a strange feeling getting on that plane in Boston and leaving my family for the first time. They were all there at Logan Airport to see me off—my parents, Uncle Vinnie, everybody; my mother really outdid herself getting ready for my first big trip.

If anybody had looked in my suitcase they'd have known the size and price of practically everything I wore because she bought me all new clothes that were still in store wrapping.

When I landed in Tampa, it was a warm night of about eighty-five degrees and I didn't know a soul when I got there. A lot of other players had landed about the same time and I got the idea they were hanging around waiting for their ride to Bradenton. It looked to me like most of them knew one another, but here I was, seventeen years old and away from home for the first time, and I remember looking up at the stars and saying, "What the heck am I doing down here?" It was a very lonely feeling.

The Red Sox sent limousines for us, and we were driven to Bradenton, where they put us in a dingy hotel. The next day at the ballpark I very luckily hitched up with a guy named Mike Ryan, who was from nearby Haverhill, Massachusetts. I could see he'd been around, and he asked me if I'd like to room with him. I said fine, and that night I moved my bags into his room at our terrible hotel. It was so terrible, in fact, that we soon moved into an apartment nearby.

The club was run by Mace Brown and Len Okrie. They told me as soon as I got there that I'd be working in the outfield, so that also told me something about my infielding. From the first day of practice, I realized I wasn't playing high-school ball anymore. It was every man for himself, and the sooner you learned this fact the better. I could see most of the guys had already spent some time in the minors before coming here and I really felt left out of it. This is why Mike Ryan was so important to me. He'd already been around for a year and he knew the score.

Right off, some of the guys tried pushing me around. I was in the batting cage one day and a player named Pete Jernigan told me to get the hell out of there. "You've had enough swings

148

already," he told me. But I'd noticed that whenever he was in the batting cage he'd swing until he was tired. So I ignored him. But he kept on me, so I finally lost my temper. I ran out of the batting cage and chased him away with my bat telling him if he didn't leave me alone I'd break it over his head. I really developed a temper down there, which only gave me more of a bear-down attitude. I realized if I ever was going to get anywhere I'd have to work extra hard because nobody gives you anything.

In my first game I singled to left field against some left-hander who wasn't throwing the ball very hard. I got a hit the next time, too, and I said to myself, "This game is easy. I got no problems." That's when I got my first taste of the slider, the good curve ball and the fastball. I'll never forget the first good curve I saw. I hit the dirt, and the umpire said it was a strike. I realized those kids down there were good and I wondered what I was doing in this company. It was too good for me. I'm sure if anybody saw the way I looked they'd have said there was no way I'd ever make the big leagues. All I can say about my hitting is that I went back to Boston with a sore thumb. I never knew a bat could vibrate so much. They did nothing but brush me back. I wasn't hitting because my left foot was facing straight out toward left field.

Actually I didn't play that much. I didn't like sitting on the bench, but I figured as long as I'm there I'd better learn by watching. At this stage of my career I was overmatched, I could see that. I realized I would have to be much stronger if I was going to make it in professional baseball. I got so depressed several times that I felt like packing my bags and going home. I wasn't doing well and I was homesick. I was so bad I was embarrassed to be there. And I guess I would have gone home if Mike Ryan hadn't been there to keep my spirits up. He told me how he had gone through the same thing the year before and that everybody does the first time.

Mike and I used to go out every night to a local meat market and buy big porterhouse steaks and take them back to the apartment for supper. One night we invited Bob Tillman and Billy MacLeod to come over and eat with us. I decided to add a dash of Italian food to the meal and volunteered to make some spaghetti. "I didn't know you could cook," Mike said.

"Sure I can," I told him. "I learned from my mother." I was stretching the truth a little bit. I'd hung around the kitchen a few times when my mother made spaghetti sauce and I figured there was nothing to it. I told them we'd be ready to eat at seven o'clock. But things ran a little late and we didn't actually sit down till ten-thirty. I put everything in the sauce but my shoes and socks—there was tomato paste, peppers, onions, oregano, salt, pepper, parsley, celery, half a chicken, and some chopped-up hamburger meat. I made enough to feed the whole Boston Army Base. Compared to my mother's sauce it was terrible; compared to anything else it was terrible.

As bad as I'd been in the Winter League it was the best thing that could have happened to me. If they'd sent me to the minors first and I'd been as bad as I was in Bradenton it would all be there in the record book. Still, it was hard for me not to feel discouraged when I got back to Boston. It had been a depressing experience for me to see how much better everybody else was. But I knew I couldn't afford to lie around the house all winter waiting for spring training to start. I just didn't have the strength in my hands and arms. So I went on a weight-lifting campaign. I bought some weights and a lead bat and I put myself on a training program. I went down to the cellar every single day in Swampscott and just worked and worked and worked. I knew what I had to do to improve myself and I did it. I didn't ever want to be embarrassed like that again.

The following spring I reported to the Red Sox minor-league base at Ocala, Florida. If I'd been in over my head at Bradenton the previous winter, I found I was back in my own class at Ocala. I really made them notice me down there. All of the Red Sox top farm people were there: Eddie Popowski, Bill Slack, Rudy York, Don Lenhardt. Lenhardt was the first guy to work with me on my fielding, and he spent more time with me than anybody else. I think he took an interest in me because he saw how hard I was trying to learn. Up to then I had played very little outfield and I quickly found out how little I really knew about it.

Lenhardt could see that I always threw three-quarter arm. That gave my ball a little tail to it. He explained to me the way the runners run in the big leagues I'd have no time to let the ball tail. He told me in the big leagues you have to throw the ball overhand all the time. He told me to hold the ball across the seams and to throw it straight over the top. He showed me how to throw, how to step, how to release the ball. It's hard to do when you've never done it before because you find you're using muscles you never used before. It took me weeks before I could throw the new way naturally. By then I had a sore arm, but I forgot about it. You don't have time for sore arms in the minor leagues if you ever want to get to the big leagues. You have to show them you want to play.

I roomed with a pitcher who had one eye. Nobody liked him, so one day I went down to the Western Union office and sent him a telegram telling him the Red Sox were pleased by his progress and he should report to Fenway Park right away. The wire told him to make his own travel arrangements, he'd be reimbursed later. The next day as we went to the cafeteria for breakfast, there he was all ready with his bags. I couldn't believe it. I knew he was obnoxious, but I didn't think he was stupid. Some of the guys dropped the news to him and he got sore as hell, saying if he ever found the guy who did this he'll kill him. He found out it was me and came after me in the room one day, but a couple of us wrestled him down and waited till he cooled off.

I sound like a big shot, but I really was lost down there. If I kidded around it was to keep the heat off me. One day I went into town to the doctor for a flu shot. There was a woman waiting there to see him. She was about forty-five years old, but she was really a good-looking woman. While we were sitting there she asked me what I did and I told her I was a ballplayer. Then she went in to see the doctor. When she came out I went in and got my shot. When I came out she was still sitting there. She told me she was waiting for me. "I have my car outside," she said. "Can I give you a lift?" I said sure, wondering what she had in mind. I soon found out: I wound up staying with her for the next two weeks.

Ocala was a melting pot for all Red Sox minor-league players. Each of us was assigned to work out with one club or another. That didn't mean you'd be playing for that club during the season. Hell, if they thought you were good enough, they'd bring you right up to the Red Sox. I had been working out with the Wellsville club which was in an A league, but I'd been hitting so well I was growing confident and I thought I had a good shot of making the Pittsfield club, which was Double-A.

Toward the end of spring training we had a roll call. "The following will report to the Pittsfield ballclub on the A diamond," a voice told us. I kept waiting to hear my name called out, but I didn't make it. Instead, I was assigned to Wellsville. I guess I was more disappointed than hurt. I didn't know it at the time, but the Red Sox had a reason for it. They wanted to put me in a league where they could build my confidence, where they thought I had a good chance of doing well. Naturally, I accepted their decision; after all, I was eager to get started in my first year of professional ball.

Just before camp broke I asked Neil Mahoney if I could go back to Boston and pick up my car before reporting to Wellsville, which is in western New York. I had just bought a 1963 Ford Galaxie convertible with my bonus money and to me that car was the living end. Mahoney said it would be all right, but cautioned me about getting there on time. He told me I'd have three days before I had to report to Wellsville and he told me not to be late.

Boy, was I late. While I was home I went over to see a girl I liked very much named Julie Makarkis. She was a cheerleader at Lynn English High School. I picked her up after school and just as we were all set to drive away, some big guy she knew jumped out in front of my car and stood there calling me the most vicious names in a loud voice. I've heard some bad language in my time, but this was the worst. The guy liked Julie and he didn't like the fact she was going off with me. He kept this up for a while and a lot of the high school kids gathered around listening.

My first inclination was to get out of the car and hit him. But Julie persuaded me not to do anything foolish. This guy stood around six foot three inches and weighed about 210 pounds, and he was the captain of the football team. So I drove off, but the guy's words really stung me. I didn't like being called names in front of all those people. I particularly didn't like having him say those things in front of Julie. After I dropped her off at her house and started for my place I said to myself, "What am I, chicken?"

I know it was a stupid thing to do, but I decided to fight him. I wasn't thinking really, because it never entered my mind how much I had to lose if I got hurt in a fight.

When I got home I put on two knee pads under my white chinos, a sweatshirt, which I cut the right sleeve off of so I could throw a right hook, a cup and jockstrap and a pair of heavy shoes. Then I drove back to Julie's house and asked her brother Alex to come with me. "I'm going over to this guy's house," I told him, "and if I get knocked out or something I want you to put me back in the car and drive me home. But I gotta fight this guy. Okay?" He agreed.

We drove to the other guy's house and I went up the stairs and knocked on his door. He saw me and knew why I was there. I was standing one step down and as he came out the door I took my right fist from practically down on the ground and I drove it upwards and smacked him right in the nose. I hit him with everything I had, and he went down bleeding heavily. I couldn't believe how hard he was bleeding. Then I ran in his house and began screaming and swearing at his mother, telling her if her son ever used that kind of language around me and a girl again I'd do the same thing all over again. Well, she started screaming back at me; she had a rolling pin in her hands she'd been using to make dough with, and she started banging me with it. I turned to leave; the guy was still down on all fours and he grabbed me around the hips. I shook him off and went back to the car, but I noticed that my white pants were now completely smeared from the waist down with his blood.

As we drove away, I felt all the tension go out of me. I felt pretty good. But I also felt a tingly feeling in my hand. I looked at my right hand and noticed the bone in my thumb was sticking right up through the skin. "I've broken my thumb right in half,

Alex," I said. What would my father say when he saw this? I didn't want to think about it.

I had to get it fixed in a hurry. I drove to a doctor I knew and he set the thumb and put it in a cast that went from the base of my thumb all the way up to my elbow. I wasn't going to be able to keep this much of a secret. I knew my whole family was at the ballfield watching my brother Billy play for Swampscott High, so I headed there. I parked the car and sent Alex looking for my Uncle Vinnie to tell him what happened. A couple of minutes later Vinnie came back with Alex. You should have seen his face when he saw me with the blood on my clothes and the cast on my hand. He busted out crying. "After all the work we've put in, now look at you," he said. I tried to tell him what happened, but I don't think he was even listening. He just looked down at that cast and shook his head. "I'd rather both my legs were broken than to have this happen to you now," he said.

I went home and got into bed. I was exhausted and humiliated and didn't want to see anybody. "What did I go and do?" I asked myself. "All my life I'm fighting for my big chance and now I have a busted thumb." When my father came home he walked into my room. He looked crushed. He stood there staring down at me on the bed and then he began calling me everything he could think of. "Look at you there," he said. "How stupid can you be? Getting in a fight now. What are you, some child? Where are your brains? You had so much more to lose than that other guy. Now what are we going to do? You make me sick." Then he walked out of the room. I lay there feeling sick and miserable. After that I guess I fell asleep. When I woke up a little later there was no pain in my thumb. Maybe it didn't happen after all, I said. Maybe it was a dream. But then I looked down and saw the cast.

The next day my father decided it would be best not to let anyone know I'd been in a fist fight. The papers would have a field day. He called up my Uncle Vinnie and told him that he was going to tell the Red Sox that I had broken my thumb while taking batting practice with him pitching to me. We'd say he threw one too close and hit me on the thumb. Vinnie agreed. Poor Uncle Vinnie, he didn't deserve this, and I hated myself for doing anything that would make him look so bad. But that's what we did. My father called Neil Mahoney and told him the story. As things turned out, I had to wear that cast for six weeks and I missed two months of what should have been my first glorious baseball season.

For one month my father didn't talk to me. I couldn't blame him. It was miserable around the house. We had just moved into a beautiful new home in Swampscott and everything should have been perfect. Instead, we had to live with this thing because I had been so damn stupid. On top of that there were serious complications with the thumb. During the six weeks I wore the cast my thumb was X-rayed by Doctor John McGillicuddy, who was the Red Sox bone specialist. I went to see him one day and he asked me, "Who set this thumb?"

I told him the doctor's name.

"I don't like it," Dr. McGillicuddy said. "This is set wrong, and it's going to take a long time to heal. The bones are overlapping."

For a while we weren't sure I'd ever be able to throw a baseball again. With the two bones overlapping I could barely open the thumb wide enough to grip a ball. There was talk of an operation or breaking the thumb again, and none of these was guaranteed to make it right. I was sent to Dr. Ed Browne, a specialist, and he didn't feel an operation would be right. He gave me a towel and told me to grab a thick part of it in my right hand;

then he told me to hold it tight in my fist and to twist it and keep twisting it. He told me to do this every chance I had. It helped stretch the thumb and I was finally able to hold a baseball. The injury also left me with a bad nerve in that hand and everytime I threw a ball it would click over the bone. I never said anything about it.

By the end of May, I was finally ready to start that long ride to Wellsville in my new Ford. It took me ten hours and two months to get there. The day I left I brought my suitcase downstairs to the kitchen. My father was there. When he saw me he broke into tears. "I'm sorry I've been so hard on you," he said. Then he wrapped his arms around me and held me close. "I'm sorry about what's happened," he said, "but you know how much I love you, how much I want you to make good. Let's forget about all that now. I want you to go there and play the hell out of that league. We both know you can do it. You know I wish you the best of luck always." When he said that I knew right there in the kitchen I was going to make the big leagues for him.

When I got to Wellsville, I realized what I'd left behind. Civilization, for one thing. It was a far throw from anything I'd ever seen before, and it was enough to convince me to work much harder so I could get out of the bush leagues. The only way to get out of places like Wellsville is to hit your way out. When I reported to the ballclub the next day, I found that all three starting outfielders were hitting well over .300. So it didn't look as if I'd be playing for a while. But the manager was Bill Slack, whom I'd met at Ocala. He told me to stay ready and not let myself get down. "You never know in this game," he told me.

There wasn't much of a hotel in Wellsville so I lived in a small house with some of the other players like Mario Pagano, Dave Casey and Bill Nagle. The town had a population of 6,000, but

I'll bet most of them were cows because only twenty-five or fifty people would show up at our games. There was one good-looking girl in town; she was a busy girl. When we weren't playing ball we had parties; they kept me from going nuts. The only good thing I felt about Wellsville was that someday I'd leave.

After a while Bill Slack began inserting me in the lineup for Homer Green, who was merely hitting .320. For a while it looked like I'd never get a hit. My first game I struck out three times in a row and don't remember even seeing the baseball. When I got back to my room that night I couldn't fall asleep. I kept lying there seeing balls whizzing past me and I couldn't get my bat around fast enough to hit them. I actually went 0–for–16 before connecting for my first hit.

It didn't take me long to find out why they're called the minors. What could be lower? Big-leaguers travel everywhere by jet, everything's air conditioned and first class. Just about the opposite is true in the minors. At Wellsville, whenever we had a road trip to make we used an old school bus that should have been retired when Calvin Coolidge was President. There were no springs in it, just solid rubber tires and a lawn mower engine. There was no way I could sleep on this thing during those beautiful four-hour trips. Conditions are so skimpy in the minors that the manager used to drive the bus.

Wellsville is in very beautiful mountainous terrain. One time we were heading for Batavia when a deer ran out in front of us and we smashed into him. The bus wouldn't start up again. We stood around for three hours hoping somebody would come along and help, but not one car came. We wound up missing a game.

The next morning a guy in a tow truck came by and got the engine working again. So we continued our trip to Batavia. But about half way there the bus broke down again. It would stall every time we had to climb a hill. So picture twenty-four ball-players dragging themselves and their equipment out and then pushing that bus up the hill. When we got to the top we'd pile back in with our stuff and ride down the hill. But as soon as we got to the bottom of another hill, we all had to get out and start pushing again. By the time we reached Batavia we were completely worn out.

In many ways playing ball under these circumstances is like being in the Army. You get tired of seeing your teammates every day and you get to dread that next long road trip in that old broken-down bus. It's bad enough getting there, but when you're through you have to turn around and start back again. On days you lose the trip is even worse. To keep the monotony from getting to us we invented different kinds of gags to play on one another. There was one played on me that has become one of the more popular ones.

They call it getting "lifted." It probably works in a variety of ways, but at Wellsville it went like this. Our equipment guy goes walking around the locker room bragging about how strong he is. He finally gets to the point where he says he can lift any three of us at the same time. Well, most of the guys know the gag and they go along with him. "Bet you can't," they say. Soon everybody is throwing money on the floor as though it's really going to be a big bet. Then the equipment guy looks around the room and picks out two guys who obviously are in on the thing. Now he needs a third, and that's when he goes looking for the patsy. This time it was me.

"Hey, Conig," he says, "you're good sized, you be the third guy." I readily agreed. We are all supposed to lie down and it's worked out that I'm the guy in the middle. We all lock arms and legs so that we are all tied pretty good together. Then the equipment guy loops several baseball belts into one and slides them under us and holds the two ends in his hands. Then he stands straddling us and begins going into his act.

"Okay, you guys," he says, "here I go." And he starts to suck in his breath for the big effort. Then he starts counting, "One . . . two . . ." Just when he says three and I expect him to make a complete fool of himself, he bends down and unzips my pants and everybody starts pulling them down and my shorts, too. Then the whole ballclub begins throwing stuff on me, whatever they've got around—shaving cream, meat from sandwiches, lettuce, pepper, everything. That's what they mean when they ask you, "Have you ever been 'lifted'?" I was "lifted." Sooner or later, everybody is.

Another joke they like to play on kids in the minors is to start by passing the word around, "There's a girl in Room 504 who's gonna take on the whole ballclub." Now not everybody on the club knows it's a gag and they can pick any one of the new kids for this one. The first time I saw it pulled I didn't know it was a gag, but luckily they had somebody else in mind.

Soon the guys begin lining up outside Room 504. I swear, at times like these ballplayers are as good as any Hollywood actors. They really make you believe. They arrange it so that the pigeon they've got in mind is somewhere up front, like fourth in line. Then the first guy goes into the room. He's there a couple of minutes. When he comes out his shirt's hanging out of his pants, his hair is messed up pretty good, and he's breathing hard. "Boy," he says, "she's great."

What he's been doing in there all that time is jumping up and down and doing pushups so he'll look like he's really been doing something. Well, this goes on with the next guy and the next.

Meanwhile, in the room we have one of our guys lying there in the dark with a handkerchief in his mouth which he uses to stifle any laughs and also to disguise his voice. Finally, it's the pigeon's turn. He's seen the other guys come out bragging and you have to figure he's more than a little bit excited. He goes in and the rest of the guys outside count up to twenty, then bust in the room and turn the lights on. The poor guy is usually embarrassed as hell.

Still, there's nothing more embarrassing than doing something wrong on the ballfield. We went to Jamestown one night for a game—the usual four-hour drag in that bus. They had a real big ballpark there; I think it was 345 down both lines and around 420 to center, so you really had to do something to hit it out of that ballpark.

I was playing center field that night and batting fourth. In the first inning I didn't get up. So I took the field. Out in center a ground ball came my way, a hit right over the bag. I came in for it and the ball went right through my legs and the hitter got three bases on it. I don't know how it got by me because I got down low for the ball, but it snuck by my glove. The next guy came up and did the same thing. A hit right up the middle and again it went under my glove for three bases. There was a big crowd there that night—which means around 1,100 people, and they really let me know about it. I was embarrassed and mad at myself.

I came into the dugout when the inning was over and I know the rest of the team thought I was crazy because I was so mad about those two balls. I started saying, "I'm gonna hit a home run on the first pitch that guy throws me. I don't care where he throws that first pitch, I'm gonna hit it out of the ballpark. He can throw it over my head, I'm gonna hit it out of the ballpark. He can throw it on the ground and I'm gonna hit it out of the ballpark. I just don't care."

When I went up there I felt like Superman; the bat felt like a toothpick in my hands. I dug in and the pitcher threw me a low fastball, and I hit that thing as high as I could to left field. As I ran toward first I lost sight of the ball because the lights in that park were so low. I didn't know where the ball was; it could have landed in left-center for all I knew. But then I saw the leftfielder looking up and the centerfielder looking up and I realized that I actually had hit a home run. When I look back on it now, I don't believe I could ever do something like that again.

I have a history of hitting home runs in unusual circumstances. The first time my father came to see me play I hit a home run at Batavia. He had made that trip with some of his cronies from back home and they followed us around for about a week. Another time he brought my mother and Richie to Wellsville and they planned on staying a week. But they got one look at that hotel and began having second thoughts about it. There was only one movie house in town and they played an Elvis Presley picture all that week. Wellsville also had one TV channel and the cable was broken the week my folks got there. So they just sat around all the time staring at each other. Richie said, "Boy, Billy was the smart one. He stayed home." After two days my father came to me and said, "Look, Choo, we love you very much. You know that. But we can't stand another minute of this." And they left. They were so in a hurry to get home my father drove ten hours nonstop.

When I finally left Wellsville I knew I'd never be going back. I batted .363 in the 83 games I played, collected 42 doubles, 4 triples, 6 stolen bases, knocked in 84 runs and hit 24 homers.

I was named both the Rookie of the Year and the Most Valuable Player in the New York–Pennsylvania League. The .363 was the highest figure anybody hit in the entire Red Sox organization. What had started out as a near-disastrous year wound up surpassing even my own wildest expectations of what my first year in organized ball would be like.

It was good to get back to Swampscott to eat some of my mother's great home cooking and to see my father strut proudly wherever he went, even if it was just a short stay. The Red Sox quickly notified me they wanted me to go to Sarasota to play in the Winter League again. Attached to this news was the fact they had added me to their 40-man roster, which meant, among other things, that I would go to spring training with them at Scottsdale, Arizona, in 1964. In those days you couldn't give me too much baseball, so I changed laundry and hopped a plane for Florida.

What a difference a year makes. The previous fall I had arrived scared and lonely, not quite sure what I'd find there or how I'd make out. Now I was a different person, I was confident. Mike Ryan was back, too, so the first thing we did was to rent a beautiful apartment on the Keys. We were a couple of veterans of this scene now.

Eddie Popowski ran the club and he worked with me every day I was down there. We spent mornings on base-running and outfield play and the more he showed me the more I realized how little I really knew. He worked me in right field all the time, hitting me low line drives I had to come in for, then sending me back to the fence for deep drives. A couple of times he brought me in to play third base just so I could learn how to short-hop the ball better. Unless you've played this game you have no idea the amount of work people like Pop do to teach kids on their way up. Don't tell me there are any natural ball-players who know it all.

In a game one day I made a couple of base-running goofs. I went from second to third on a ground ball hit right at the short-stop, and Pop later explained to me that I should have stayed at second. I also tried to score from third on a ground ball with a drawn-in infield. I was a dead duck at the plate. Pop told me I should have let myself get trapped in a rundown play so that the other runners could move up on the bases. I listened and nodded, and knew I wouldn't blow plays like that again. As for my hitting, the pitchers didn't bother me this time. I hit .258 in 34 games and got 4 homers.

When I got home in December I was bristling with confidence. I couldn't wait for March and spring training. I was a month shy of my nineteenth birthday and I was thinking of my chances of making the Red Sox the next season. They had finished in seventh place in 1963, so obviously they needed better ballplayers. I was one of four kids they had put on the roster (the others were Tony Horton and pitchers Dave Gray and Pete Charton) and the rules then said they would have to carry three of us all season or risk losing us in the draft. I told my father I could be one of those three.

He could see how high I was and tried to calm me down. At supper one night he said, "Look, Choo, I just wonder if you wouldn't be better off going to the minors next season and play-ing every day, rather than sticking with the Red Sox and sitting on the bench."

I said, "Dad, I can make that club. Look at the outfield. Who do I have to beat out? There's Yastrzemski. That's all. The other guys are Lou Clinton, Roman Mejias, and Gary Geiger. Why can't I go into one of those spots?"

"Well, don't count on it too much," my father said. "I wouldn't want you to be too disappointed if you don't make it."

"Look Dad," I went on, "I'm coming back with the club next spring. You'll see."

"I hope so," he said. "But don't get your hopes up too high. You are only nineteen and you've had just one year of pro ball behind you."

"I'm not," I said. "But I'm gonna work hard and make that club, and I tell you I'm not gonna sit on the bench, either."

I spent the rest of that winter working out every day down in our basement. I lifted weights and swung that lead bat till my hands were raw. I read in the papers that Mike Higgins, the Red Sox general manager who had scouted me when I was playing Legion ball, had seen me in Sarasota and was telling the writers I reminded him of young Al Kaline. I felt strangely confident and by the end of February I had my mind made up that I wasn't going to Scottsdale to be overlooked. There was a place on the roster for me and I was going to make sure somebody noticed me.

Let me tell you about Scottsdale. I have never seen anything like it before. It was cool, cool in a way that your eye could travel for what seemed hundreds of miles and you could see pink desert and orange mountains. The ballclub stayed at the Ramada Inn, which was beautiful and neat, and about a million miles away from Wellsville. My old friend, Tony Horton, who had beaten me out of all that bonus money, was assigned as my roommate. We were both bachelors, we both liked girls and we were to have some good times down there.

Even though we trained with the big ballclub, that didn't make for instant friendships. Mostly, the veterans stayed by themselves and did their best to let the rest of us know they didn't know we were around. I could see guys like Yastrzemski, Dick Stuart, Bill Monbouquette, and Dick Radatz, but they didn't know I was alive. This kind of situation changed very gradually.

One of my first days there I came walking out of the dugout to loosen up. I wasn't looking where I was going. Suddenly, a ball came flying right for my head and I hit the dirt. I got up, looked around to see who threw it at me and saw Dick Williams, one of the veterans. He yelled out at me, "Watch where you're going, bush." I don't remember seeing him smile when he said it.

The next day I was out playing catch with Dick Stuart and I saw Williams coming out of the dugout. He wasn't looking where he was going and I fired a ball right at his head. Down he went, his cap flying off his head, and there was dust all over him. "Watch where you're going, bush," I yelled at him. Williams got up and I could see he was mad. He started coming for me. This was a guy who'd been around a couple of years and he probably could have done a job on me. I still weighed around 176 pounds. But as he got close, Dick Stuart said to him, "Watch where you're going, bush," and he shoved him away. That was the first friendly thing a veteran ballplayer ever did for me, and after that Stuart and I became real close friends. We'd go out to dinner and he told me everything he knew about the pitchers in our league. As for Dick Williams, we just never hit it off after that incident.

I'll never forget when Ted Williams came to camp. There had been talk all winter that he might be going off on a hunting safari to New Zealand that might prevent him from coming to the Red Sox camp, and I was disappointed. I'd always wanted to meet him and get some batting tips from him. But he came, arriving the day our manager, Johnny Pesky, had scheduled a game between the veterans and the rookies. I had seen Ted only once before close up, and that was at Ocala the year before. He hit me fly balls for a couple of hours and I'll tell you there is nobody in this whole world better than Ted at hitting the ball and making you run for it, but keeping it just out of your reach. In Scottsdale, he had my tongue hanging out. Just before he hit me one he yelled out, "See if you can catch this one, bush, and I'll give you a Cadillac." I yelled back, "I already have a Cadillac." Which, of course, was a big fat lie. It didn't matter. I never got to the ball.

The night before our game with the veterans I told Tony Horton I wasn't going out that night. "I'm going to get plenty of sleep," I said. "I want to be strong and ready tomorrow." So I got into bed and I slept for thirteen hours. In the game we bombed the veterans by a 5–0 score with Horton, Rico Petrocelli, and me all hitting homers. Williams had arrived early, slipped into a uniform and watched the game. When it was over Pesky told Horton, Rico, Dick Stuart, Dalton Jones, and me to stick around for extra batting practice so Williams could watch us. When I came out of the cage Ted called me over and said, "Don't change that solid stance of yours, no matter what you're told." Having Ted Williams, to me the greatest hitter of all time, say a thing like that really boosted my confidence. He also told me that in a week or so he'd sit down and talk hitting with me, telling me about the different pitchers in the American League and how to handle them. To me he was the president, period.

Later on I heard that Ted Williams told some writers he felt I was still two years away from making the majors. I accepted that. But that didn't mean I was going to let up any. I played as hard as I could every time I had a chance to get into the lineup.

We opened the exhibition season against the Cubs in Mesa. I was on the bench. I had been hitting the ball good in camp games and I really thought I deserved to play, but Pesky started Lou

Clinton in right field. We were trailing, 4–0, in the sixth inning when he sent me in to replace Clinton. When I came to bat in the seventh I hit a long foul down the line in left, then struck out. But I came up in the ninth and singled to start a three-run rally. We still lost the game, 6–4.

This was the pattern for the next several games. Clinton would start the ballgame and I'd go in as a late-inning replacement. But I'd get a hit nearly every day, and I was handling fly balls very well and making the right throws. I kept thinking back to Don Lenhardt driving me all the time about doing things the right way. And now it was beginning to pay off. After I'd had a couple of good days the writers began asking Pesky if I had a chance to stick with the club. He said I sure did. He liked the way I was fielding, but he told them, "He's got a lot of base hits to get between now and April 14."

I guess Pesky had his reasons for playing me. The vets weren't hitting, and we were losing. The team was short of outfielders. Aside from Clinton, Mejias, and Dick Williams they had nobody else with experience. They'd been hoping Gary Geiger would get to camp in time, but he was still recuperating from an ulcer operation. So I was getting my chance to play and I was getting my hits.

About two weeks into the exhibition season Pesky gave me my first chance to start. We were playing the Indians at Tuscon and he decided to start a whole rookie lineup with the exception of starting pitcher Bill Monbouquette. We beat them, 5–4, and I collected 3 doubles, getting two of them by stretching ordinary singles and going into the bag with good slides. I know I opened some eyes that day. Funny thing is I almost didn't start that game. The flight into Tuscon from El Paso was bumpy and I became air sick. I spent that whole flight with my face in my hands but I wasn't going to ask to be taken out.

Against the Giants the next day I got two more hits, including a 370-foot double against the fence off Billy Pierce, and I believe I was now the hottest hitter in camp. About this time Pesky decided to play me in center because Mejias wasn't hitting. When I got back to Scottsdale I found I had received about twenty-five or thirty fan letters, my first fan mail, and I couldn't believe it. I sat down that night and began answering every one of them.

A couple of days later my parents arrived from Boston. Boy, was I glad to see them. My mother had never flown on a plane before, so I never even thought they'd come. But a few nights earlier my folks had some people over to the house and everyone began saying wouldn't it be nice if they could come to see me. They'd been reading stories in the papers and they wanted to see for themselves. My father got my mother in a weak moment and she said all right, she'd fly. The next day she regretted having said it, but it was too late. My father had already bought the tickets. When they got to Scottsdale I got them a nice room at the Ramada Inn.

Their first day in Scottsdale we had a game scheduled against the Indians and they were sitting down in the third-base area. I didn't start. We were trailing, 5–3, in the seventh when Pesky sent me to right field. The next inning I came up, there was nobody on and Gary Bell was pitching for the Indians. He could really throw smoke in those days. His first pitch was a ball. Then he threw me a letter-high fastball and I came around on it, but good. I cracked it high and far toward dead center field and to my own amazement saw it disappear over the wall for a home run. It didn't hit me right then, but I had hit this ball better than

169

430 feet; I later learned that I'd become the first hitter ever to clear that fence. All I could think of at that moment was that my folks were there and I'd hit this homer for them. As I came around third base I waved to them. Yeah, just like in the movies, but I really did.

Later on Larry Claflin, who writes for the Boston *Record American,* actually went out to measure the distance of the drive. He said it went 560 feet, and the ball must have been as high as thirty feet in the air. Some people called it the longest home run ever hit in the state of Arizona, and to this day I still hear about it. As a matter of fact, when Claflin got out there a couple of witnesses showed him where they had seen the ball land, and I've been told it actually carried 572 feet.

After spending a week with me, my folks went off to visit some friends in Las Vegas before returning to Boston. While they were in Scottsdale my father had become pretty friendly with Johnny Pesky and in fact they and their wives had dinner together one night. But my father steered clear of talking about me. He would never discuss me with Pesky because he was afraid of how it might look. But on the day they left, he was sitting around the pool with Pesky and my father was busting. He thought I was doing great, but he had no idea what was on Pesky's mind. Finally he blurted out, "For Christ sake, John, what are you going to do about Tony?"

"What do you mean what am I going to do with him?" Pesky said. "He's my starting centerfielder, that's what he is. Put that in your pipe and smoke it."

Pesky also gave me the news. It was going to be Yaz in left, me in center, and Lou Clinton in right on opening day in Yankee Stadium. It made my flesh tingle when he told me. Johnny Pesky gave me my big-league career. There aren't many managers who will take a chance on a nineteen-year-old kid in only his second year of organized ball. Sure, I know, I hit very well down there. I had batted .308 and got 16 hits in exhibition games; only 3 of them were singles. I led the ballclub with 4 homers, had 11 runs-batted-in and a slugging percentage of .750. But lots of rookies do that and then fail when the team goes north. But John always had faith in me. He really could have sent me down if he wanted to and nobody would have blamed him. I'm happy to say that John and his wife Ruthie later became our neighbors in Swampscott.

Scottsdale was also the place where Tony Horton and I got our first taste of big-league women. We used to go down at night to a club called J.D.'s. The first time we went there to make the rounds we saw a lot of girls, but we weren't sure what they were like. To play it on the safe side we invited eight different girls to come to our room the next night. I mean we'd meet two of them, get friendly and then invite them back. We really weren't sure they meant it when they said they would come. So we kept on asking all the girls we liked and wound up inviting eight of them over. We told them we were having a little party. But we didn't invite any other ballplayers because we weren't sure any of the girls would show.

About seven o'clock the next night there was a knock at the door. We opened the door and it was two of the girls. They came in and we put on the record player and started dancing and having a good time. A couple of minutes later there was another knock. Tony and I figured out it must be some more girls, so we asked the two with us if they'd mind very much hiding in the closet because we told them it was probably our manager and we weren't supposed to have girls in the room. So they hid and we opened the door. It was two more girls.

171

We didn't know what to tell these girls, except that we weren't supposed to have any girls in the room so to please be very quiet. Tony and I, you have to understand, were both just a little crazy. So we started dancing with these two girls when there was another knock on the door. So we told these girls the same thing we had told the first two. We got them to go out on the patio and we drew the curtains.

Sure enough it was another set of girls. We invited them in and asked them to sit down. I was sure the girls in the closet had figured things out by now but they were too embarrassed to come out. Five minutes later the last set showed up. We told the two with us to get under the bed. So now we had three different sets of girls hiding around the place and a fourth set at the door. We went through the same routine with them, when all of a sudden, Tony and I started laughing and we both became hysterical over this crazy scene. Well, the two girls standing there asked us what was so funny. Then Tony said, "O.K. Everybody out!" The two girls under the bed came out and started screaming at us, and the two in the closet came out and started doing the same thing. Meanwhile, Tony and I couldn't stop laughing; he went to the patio, slid open the doors and shouted, "Come on in."

I guess I realized after that when you're a major-league ballplayer and you ask a girl out, she'll go.

The only sad part about all this was that when the team started north, Tony was the rookie they elected to option out. He'd had a very good year in 1963 at Waterloo, batting .283 and hitting 21 homers. But they now wanted to make him into a first-baseman, so they shipped him to Reading. I not only lost a roommate, but I lost a good friend. In the years since then, I've come to realize how fleeting some of these friendships are. You get close to a

guy, then the ballclub trades him away and you don't see each
other anymore. This happened a little later on with Mike Ryan
when the Red Sox sent him to Philadelphia. It's part of baseball.
It's better when you're a kid and dream of being in the big
leagues. But when you're there, you have to accept whatever
they throw at you, whether you like it or not. As soon as Tony
Horton left, I was assigned to room with Frank Malzone, the
third-baseman. He's a great guy and I probably would have
enjoyed myself. But Frank was an older player and sometime
after the season started, he switched to one of the guys his own
age. So I got another roommate: his name was Dick Williams.
We had barely talked to one another at Scottsdale, as a result
of our little throwing exchange, and now they were putting us
in the same bedroom.

No two people were ever more unalike than Williams and I.
How anyone arranged our rooming together I'll never know.
Big-league clubs like to room rookies with vets so the kids will
have someone to learn from, and Williams was always regarded
as a good company man; so that could be the reason they put us
together. He had once been a fairly promising outfielder with
the Brooklyn Dodgers. One day he landed on his throwing
shoulder while coming in for a fly ball and he wrecked it. He
never could really throw again, so he spent the next thirteen years
or so as a very good utility ballplayer who could fill in at any
position. Now he was a married man with kids who called his
wife on the phone every night and he looked at me as some bush
kid, and there was no way we could get together. We finally
agreed we had enough of each other and I moved in with a
young pitcher named Ed Connolly. Nobody would have suspected that in just three years Williams would be the Red Sox
manager.

Opening day of 1964 it rained in New York and the game was postponed. When I woke up in my room in the Commodore the next day, it was still raining and I was sure the game would be called off again. I went back to sleep. A little later the phone rang and it was Fitzy. "What the hell's the matter with you?" he said. "Where are you?"

"What do you mean, where am I?" I said. "I'm here in my hotel room. I'm sleeping."

"Well, the whole ballclub's here working out," Fitzy said, "and you're the only one that's missing."

Oh, my God. I was getting off on the wrong foot again. Frank Malzone, who was rooming with me, had gone home to the Bronx and I'd completely forgotten that Pesky had told us he wanted everybody at the Stadium whether the game was on or off. At times like that you can think of the giddiest things, and the thought that ran through my head was that some day one of my grandchildren would ask me what it was like going to Yankee Stadium the first time and I would say, "I don't know. I overslept that day."

I really had no time for funny answers; I had no time even for a shower. I threw my clothes on as fast as I could and raced downstairs and got a cab. Halfway across the bridge leading to Yankee Stadium, the cab got a flat tire. I began screaming at the poor driver and he didn't know what was the matter with me. So I left, got another cab, and finally showed up at the Stadium about an hour late. The first thing I found out was that Pesky was fining me $10, which was an automatic club rule. I figured I got off cheap, but when the writers came around later and asked me about it I told them it should have been $1,000. I said it, but I sure didn't mean it. A thousand dollars is a lot of money

174

especially when all you're making is $7,500, but I figured it would show that I took this thing seriously, which I did.

Finally, the next day the weather was all right and we opened against the Yankees. When I stepped on that field the first time that day, I was awed just by being there in Yankee Stadium. It was about as thrilling and exciting a moment for me as I can ever recall. My parents and brothers were all there, and so were a lot of friends from Boston who had flown down to see me play my first major-league game. Here I was, nineteen years old, less than two years out of high school; last year at this time I was supposed to be on my way to Wellsville, and now, all of a sudden, here I was in Yankee Stadium.

If all this wasn't enough, I was starting my first game against two guys I had idolized all my life, Mickey Mantle and Whitey Ford. When our team went out in order in the first inning, I started running out toward center field. I saw Mantle coming my way. We were going to pass each other around second base and I honestly froze. What would I say to him, I asked myself. Mickey made it easy. As he got close he just said, "Hi, kid, How're you doing?" Great. Now we're pals. I just said, "Fine," and kept on running to my position.

Bill Monbouquette was pitching for us. I looked around me and saw the biggest center field I had ever seen in my life. Joe DiMaggio had spent his entire career out here and was supposed to have made every catch look easy. It seemed impossible, and I felt pretty small standing there while Mombo warmed up. Phil Linz stepped in for the Yankees and hit Mombo's first pitch, a high fly ball straight at me. It was an easy chance and I made it look routine. But my heart was pounding.

When we came off the field, I was due up third. Dick Stuart

175

and Lou Clinton got on base. As I came up for my first time at bat, there was Whitey Ford standing on the mound. I dug in. I told myself I didn't care who was out there, just take your normal cut, which in my case, is always as hard as I can do it. I nearly hit into a triple play. I banged the ball down hard right at Clete Boyer at third base. He grabbed it, stepped on the bag, and fired across to Bobby Richardson at second for the force; I barely beat his throw to Joe Pepitone at first base. I told the writers later I was eager to get into the record books, but I didn't want to make it that way.

In the second inning, Tommy Tresh hit one to deep right-center. It looked like it would hit the wall and go for extra bases. I dug back as fast as I could; the ground felt soggy after two days of rain, but I managed to move pretty well. At the 407-sign I looked up and was blinded by the sun. So I raised my glove to shade my eyes and the ball plopped in. For a split second I didn't even know I had caught it. The fans gave me a big round of applause, and I tried to behave as though I made catches like that every day.

My next time up against Ford I singled for my first major-league hit, but what I did my third time up at bat got a lot more space in the papers the next day. Ford threw me a pitch which landed in front of the plate and bounced off the catcher's chest. I reached down to pick it up and noticed there was a big blotch of mud on the ball. The ground around home plate was dry and dusty because they had kept it covered with a tarpaulin before the game. So I put two and two together and concluded Ford must have thrown me a spitter.

"For crying out loud," I said to the umpire, "why don't you make him wipe that stuff off the ball before he throws it?" The umpire looked at me funny, took the ball and just scraped all the mud off, and then threw it back to Ford. He never said a word. We beat Ford that day, 4–3, but the big story after the game was how I had opened up my big mouth and accused Whitey Ford of throwing a spitter. The thing went coast to coast and I was made out to be a cocky kid.

Now it was home to Boston for our own opener. I don't think I was nervous; anxious would be the way I felt. I got a good night's sleep and the next morning went to Fenway Park at ten o'clock. I wanted to learn whatever I could about center field there. One of our coaches, Harry Malmberg, hit me fly balls for about an hour, banging shots off the wall so I could learn how to handle the rebounds. Then all I had to do was go back to the clubhouse and wait for the game to start.

During pregame batting and fielding practice I stayed pretty much by myself. I just wanted to concentrate on the game. I knew it was not time for making small talk. When practice was over I went back to the clubhouse to change into some dry things. We were playing the Chicago White Sox that day and Joe Horlen was pitching for them. From the stack of maybe 100 telegrams in my locker you'd have thought I had changed places with Yaz. But I had a lot of friends and family pulling for me and they were wishing me well. As game time got nearer I began to hope this day was over already, even though I had waited all my life for it to happen.

Fenway was packed. There was a big gallery of celebrities there, from Bobby and Ted Kennedy and their family to the Governor of Massachusetts and the Mayor of Boston, Stan Musial, Jack Dempsey and Gene Tunney, Carol Channing and Frederic March; they were all there because the game was dedicated to the late President John F. Kennedy. The rest of the people were mine—old teammates, friends, and family. There were my mother and father, Billy and Richie, my Uncle Vinnie and Aunt Phyllis, my grandmother, Ben Campbell. I'd say the Conigliaros outnumbered the Kennedys that day.

When I came up for my first at-bat in the second inning my people let me know they were there. Horlen's first pitch to me was a waist-high fastball and I went right after it. It soared on a high arc for the left-field screen, but as I watched it while running down the line I knew it wasn't going to land on the screen. I knew it was going clear over it, right onto Landsdowne Street. I put my head down and circled the bases. This was no time to miss a bag or do something stupid. I guess I did everything right because when I got back to the dugout they were all standing up and clapping their hands. This time I decided it wouldn't be right to go looking for my folks up in the stands, though I knew exactly where they were.

Later on a mailman who had been passing the spot where my homer hit the ground came to the clubhouse and gave the ball to me. I autographed another ball and gave it to him. The writers asked me if I'd gone up there with the idea of hitting the first pitch. I told them no, but that I go up there with the intention of hitting the first good pitch I see. "I don't like to give the pitcher any kind of edge," I told them.

I got off to the kind of start that surprised everyone, including myself. After a month of the season I was hitting .270 and had collected 5 homers, 3 doubles, a triple, and 11 runs-batted-in. I slumped for several days but then picked up again and got hits in 10 of the next 11 games, which was a .364 pace. Pesky was impressed and amazed. He also could see I was experiencing a little difficulty in center field. Until he had put me out there in spring training I had never played the position before, and he was afraid the pressure might build up and affect my hitting. So he

178

asked Yaz to trade positions with me. I was far more comfortable in left.

The 1964 season seemed to set a pattern for what so far has been my big-league career. I've been out with injuries a lot, mostly from getting hit by pitches. Maybe it's the way I crowd the plate, but that's the way I hit and I've never let any pitcher discourage me. But if they didn't discourage me, they sidelined me. In May, Moe Drabowsky hit me in the left wrist. He said he wasn't trying to brush me back, and I guess that's so. In my three previous times against him that day he pitched me outside, so naturally, I thought he was coming outside again. Only this time he tried to fool me by jamming me with a fastball and that's how I got hit. I was lucky it was a hairline fracture and I was only out for a week.

A month later I wasn't so lucky. We were in Comiskey Park and I went back to the cement wall for a drive down the line by Ron Hansen. At the last second, I tried to make a backhand catch and missed. I toppled over the short brick wall and fell unconscious in the seats. I was carried off on a stretcher and came to in the clubhouse. Somebody asked me if I knew who I was, but I was too dazed to answer. This time I had bursitis in the left knee, a swollen right hand and an injured back. I was out nine days.

A month later we were in Cleveland. I knew a girl named Peggy Fleming (not *the* Peggy Fleming), and after a day game on Saturday she invited the announcer Curt Gowdy and me to come out to her house to a party her parents were throwing. Curt was an old friend of the family. He couldn't make it, but I wanted to go. I didn't have a car, so she came into town and picked me up. At the party I was having a pretty good time, but around eleven o'clock I told the Flemings I had to get back to town to make midnight curfew. The party was still going strong and they asked me to stay overnight; after all, it wasn't as if I was out carousing. That was my first mistake, accepting their hospitality, nice as it was. My second mistake was in not calling Pesky at the hotel and checking with him. By midnight I was in bed. The next morning the Flemings drove me to Municipal Stadium where we had a doubleheader scheduled with the Indians.

When I walked into the clubhouse I could feel the rest of the guys quiet down. Fitzy came over and said Pesky wanted to see me. I wasn't late so I figured it had to do with the night before. I went in and Pesky told me off pretty good. Of course, he didn't know why I was not in my room the night before and he couldn't have cared. "It's going to cost you $250," he said. I swallowed. That was a good-sized fine, the biggest he'd ever handed out. I couldn't blame John, but he did give me a chance to tell my story. Then he said, "The fine sticks."

I did not protest the fine, because I realized that he now was on the spot. He has always been a nice human being, one of the finest men I have ever known; we are good friends today. John was a ballplayer's manager, the kind who never could hurt anyone. Maybe a manager shouldn't be that way, but that's how John was. The writers were saying discipline was one of the problems with the Red Sox. So even if John wanted to excuse me for some rookie foolishness, consider his position. Besides, he had warned me earlier in the season about not breaking curfew, so I can't even say he treated me unfairly. He even tried to keep the fine a secret from the writers.

That started my day. In the first game I came up and belted a three-run homer off Lee Stange. It was my twentieth of the year, and people were saying at that pace I could come close to 40, or at least break the rookie record of 38. As I got back to the dugout I looked John's way, but he pretended not to see me. "Are you still gonna fine me?" He didn't answer. He was still plenty angry. We won the ballgame, 6–1. In the second game we were facing Pedro Ramos. I came up in the third inning and hit a deep shot that looked sure to be No. 21, but Vic Davalillo raced back and made a sensational catch to rob me just as it was going over the barrier.

This was an especially bright day and the sun had a glare to it that made the ball hard to pick out. I remember Dick Stuart almost caught one of Ramos' fastballs in the head and he came back to the dugout saying, "That's it. I'm not digging in against him today. I couldn't see that ball." That should have given me a warning, but I am difficult to reach on occasion.

My next time up Ramos threw one in close. I couldn't pick it out and the ball hit me on the right arm. I dropped to the ground in agony. Our trainer, Jack Fadden, came out of the dugout and said, "Here, let me have a look at it, Tony." But I told him right away, "Forget it, Jack. I've got a broken arm." When I was taken to the hospital it was confirmed: a broken ulna. The forecast was that I'd be out six to eight weeks, maybe for the rest of the year. This killed me. I'd been hitting a ton and the club was playing .500 ball. Now it looked as if I was through for the season. They put a cast on my arm and I went home.

Of course, at a time like this a lot of the Boston writers thought it was far more important to improve my image as a playboy, and many of the stories about me neglected the broken arm or the 20 homers I'd hit and instead talked about the night life I was supposed to be leading. The girl I had seen in Cleveland was all of sixteen years old, just a kid of sixteen, and I was at her house with her family all night. If I was looking to be a playboy, I certainly could have done a better job than that.

In September I was ready to play again. Pesky sent me up to pinch-hit in my first game back and I homered. I got back in the lineup and hit three more homers. When the season was over, I had a .290 batting average with 24 homers and 52 runs-batted-in. I would have had a good shot at 30 and probably would have made it, if it hadn't been for the injuries. All together, I was out of the lineup on six different occasions and played in 111 ball-games.

All in all, it was a satisfying year. Looking back on it now, I'd say 1964 was my happiest year. I had comparatively little trouble with the press, and the fans were just great. This was to change swiftly in 1965.

During the off-season I attended a press luncheon at Fenway Park. Mike Higgins was there and felt it might be a good time to discuss my 1965 contract with him. I had made $7,500 as a rookie, which was the major-league minimum then, and I felt I had proved something with my 20 homers and other contributions. The club had already sent me a contract offering me $9,000, but I felt it was far short of what I deserved.

When the lunch was over I said to him, "Mike, if you have a few minutes, let's talk over my contract."

Mike was a big man with a soft voice. He looked at me like he wasn't sure he'd heard me right, but he said, "Weren't you happy with it?"

"No," I said. "I wasn't."

He paused again before answering, then finally said, "Well, all right. If you want to talk, let's go down to my office."

We walked out on the roof of Fenway, down a flight of stairs and into his office. "Well," Mike said, "what's it all about?"

"I want more money," I told him.

"I thought we were fairly generous," Mike said.

"No, it isn't enough," I said. "I want more."

He looked a little annoyed with me. "Now look, Tony," he said. "You still have to prove yourself. You just had one year up here. You do well next season and we'll make it up to you. You'll see."

"I'm not interested in next year, Mike," I told him. "I had a pretty good year this year, and I think I deserve more than $9,000."

He got up from his desk and began to pace. His face was beginning to look a little angry. "Tell you what," Mike said after another long pause. "The best we can do—and I'm doing you a favor—is $12,000." Then, without waiting for an answer from me, he turned and called to his secretary, "Mary, make up a contract for Tony for $12,000."

"Hey, wait a minute, Mike," I said. "No, I'm not going to sign for $12,000. I want more than that."

"Look Tony," he said. "If you were working in a factory you'd never get an increase like that. That's $4,500. I can't go any higher than that. Why don't you just settle?"

"No, Mike," I said.

He was really agitated now and I wondered if I could keep it up much longer. He looked at me and said, "Well, you must have some figure in your mind. How much do you want?"

"$17,500," I said.

I thought he'd choke. "You've got to be kidding," he said. "What are you, insane? There's no way I can do that. The club would object. The owner would object." He paused again and paced. He sat down and began scrawling on a pad of paper in front of him. "Tell you what," he said. "I'll make it $14,000. That's the best I can do." He turned again and without waiting for me to say something he called out, "Hey, Mary. Draw up a contract for Tony Conig . . ."

"Hey, wait a minute," I said. "No, I'm not signing for that."

"That's as far as I'm going to go," Mike said.

"Look, don't you want me to be a happy ballplayer?" I said. "I'm from Boston. If I play well, we'll be drawing more people. You'll see."

"Who the hell do you think you are?" he said.

"Well, I'm not signing for $14,000," I said. "If you don't want to argue, just come up with another $3,500."

He got up and began pacing again. "Well, I'm crazy," Mike said. "But I'm going to do it. Hey, Mary. Draw up a contract for Tony Conigliaro for $17,500." This time I didn't attempt to stop him. Then Mike said, "We're really proud of you, Tony. We want you to be happy. Do a good job for us."

While waiting for the contract to be finished, I tried to look nonchalant, but my heart was really pounding. After signing it, I ran downstairs, got in my car, closed all the windows and then began screaming at the top of my lungs. I couldn't believe it. I was offered $9,000 and I talked it up to $17,500. I drove off looking for a phone booth; I had to tell my father. I found one on the roadside and called him at work. When he heard the news he let out a big yell, too. Then I drove off for the house. On my way, I thought to myself, maybe I could have got him up to $30,000. Who knows?

The Red Sox were an eighth-place ballclub in 1964, which I think was no fault of Johnny Pesky's. I've always believed he was a much better manager than he showed. But you can't do anything when you don't have the ballplayers, and we didn't have them. Pesky was fired and replaced by Billy Herman, but things were even worse in 1965 under Herman. That was the year a lot of things happened to me that pretty much established my baseball image: I proved myself as a home-run hitter; I got

myself in hot water with the writers; I couldn't get along with
Billy Herman.

It's hard to say how these last two things got started. I was a
kid of nineteen, much wetter behind the ears than I'd admit, and
I always said whatever came into my mind. If a writer asked me
a question, I gave him an answer as quick as I could get it out,
and the next thing I knew I'd be reading it in print. Now in
some cities, if a player isn't smart enough to protect himself, the
writers protect him. Not in Boston, which has always been very
competitive because of all the different papers and the writers
fighting one another for scoops. So I learned the hard way that if
I said something stupid, I could bet it would appear in the paper
the next day.

Having a losing ballclub helped. It's one thing when you're
winning and fighting for a pennant; the writers have plenty of
good copy. But when you're losing and playing bad baseball,
they go looking for stuff other than baseball. I've never been able
to understand why they have to know what I think of this or
that girl. I've always felt baseball writers should report baseball.
But that's their business. It was this whole combination of things
plus the fact that Billy Herman and I were on different wave
lengths that led to my many troubles in 1965.

I had been telling the writers in spring training that I didn't
believe in any soph jinx, that I'd had mine as a rookie with all my
injuries. Still, I got off to a pretty bad start when the season
opened. I was hitting home runs, but my average was down and
I started getting it from the fans. I realized how the same people
who can be with you one day can turn around the next and call
you whatever comes into their minds, and I heard some pretty
awful things out there in right field during my slump. I was hurt
and confused; it was something I'd never run into before. One

day I blurted out in the clubhouse that they were the worst fans in baseball, and the next day the Boston papers quoted me very accurately. Of course, I didn't mean all of the fans, just those using that foul language, but the writers were only too happy to have a good story and not one of them gave me a chance to back out a little bit.

In June, everyone I knew thought he understood what I was doing wrong and wanted to share it with me. I was told I was moving my feet, dropping my hands, stepping wrong, pulling my head up before swinging. Even my milkman was giving me batting tips.

I knew I was swinging for home runs too much. Mike Higgins mentioned this to me and got me to promise him I'd swing for base hits for a while till my stroke returned. I did and things began to straighten out. I got my average back up to around .270 and I had 10 homers. Once I felt I had licked the slump, I realized how much my mental attitude mattered. You have to keep believing you're going to snap out of it and never stop trying.

Then I ran into another streak which had very little to do with the way I played ball. It began on a road trip in July and very nearly ended with my being sent back to the minor leagues. We were in Washington and one night after a game I took out a girl I knew. I got back to my hotel room about twenty minutes after curfew, and Mike Ryan told me that Herman had phoned a few minutes earlier. I called Billy's room and he said I was going to be fined for being out after hours. "Billy," I said, "for being late twenty minutes?"

"That's right," he said. "You weren't in your room on time, were you?"

"No," I said. "But Billy, it was only twenty minutes. Will the papers find out?"

"Yes, I guess they will," he answered. He heard my groan and said, "All right, look. You're being fined. But if the writers ask you about it, tell them no, you were in your room on time."

Which I did, because the next morning word was all over the hotel that a lot of the players had broken curfew and were being fined. When Clif Keane asked me if I was one of them I denied it. But some of the guys who'd been out knew I had broken curfew, too, and they branded me a liar. Herman failed to back me up, and the stories sent back to Boston called me a liar.

A couple of days later, we were flying to Cleveland for a series. The previous winter I had cut a rock-and-roll record which sold out in Boston, and I had begun carrying a portable record player with me so I could hear music on road trips. I was listening to music in the back of the plane with Rico, Tony Horton, and Jerry Stephenson. One of the older players went up front to Herman, who was playing cards with some of the writers, and told him about the music.

Now Herman probably had his reasons for being sore at me. I was in another slump, which had brought my average down to .257, and while I already had hit 16 homers, I hadn't hit one in a couple of weeks. So Billy said, "I wonder how that thing would sound on a bus between Toronto and Toledo." The Red Sox had a farm team at Toronto and he was implying he could send me back to the minors.

When we got to Cleveland, I found my name wasn't in the starting lineup. For the first time in my career, I was benched, and I felt humiliated. As soon as I was in uniform, I ran out on the field, and even though it was raining, I jogged in the outfield for about twenty minutes. The rain was pelting down on me but I was angry and trying to clear my head. When I got back to the locker room to dry off, Henry McKenna, who covers the Red Sox for the *Herald,* asked me what was up. I was so steamed off, I let it all out of my system.

"Baseball is everything in my life," I told him, "and it looks like somebody's trying to get rid of me." Then I said, "I'm so down in the dumps I can't get out of it. I don't know what to do. I'm really hurt." I mentioned the record player and that my mother had called me on the phone and asked me not to play it if it was going to bother Herman. I said I wouldn't play it anymore. "All of these stories about me not trying to help the team are unfair," I went on. "Sure I've struck out a lot, but I've also hit some good shots. What about the single last night that tied the game? It's nice to get a pat on the back, but I never get one. Never."

After going on like this for a while, I felt better. I looked over at McKenna and saw him writing away like crazy. I said to him, "Look, I'm teed off at Herman for benching me. Maybe I said a lot of things I shouldn't have said. Would you not use that stuff?" Now, I know he had a right to use anything he heard me say but I would have hated his guts for printing it. But I saw him take his pencil and seem to cross out whatever he had put down. He made it look to me like it was all off the record.

The benching lasted only one game. But the damage of what I had said to McKenna would haunt me for a lot longer. McKenna printed almost everything I had told him. I found this out when my father telephoned me in New York a couple of days later to ask me if I was crazy. He told me how Boston headlines were featuring stories on how I was rocking-and-rolling my way back to the minors. On the flight from Cleveland to New York, I had even gone up to Herman in the front of the plane and asked him if it was all right to play my records. He said, "No, I don't mind, just as long as it's after a winning game." Well, we had just beaten the Indians, 4–1, so I played them.

During our series in New York, Tony Horton came up to me after one of the games and said, "How'd you like to go to a party? I know about a place where there must be a hundred stewardesses living." I said, "Sure, what are we waiting for? Let's get dressed." I had had a couple of beers right after the game. It's not that I liked the taste much, but Jack Fadden had told me it would help keep my weight up, so I usually had a couple after every game. When Tony and I left, I was already feeling pretty good.

When we walked into the party, neither of us could believe what we saw. There must have been six girls to every guy in the room, and every girl was beautiful. I didn't know which way to turn, and before I knew it, Tony was moving around pretty well. I began doing the same thing, talking to a girl for a few minutes, then my head would be turned by another and I'd be off talking to her. I found a pencil and paper and began getting the phone number of every girl I could. I felt like a kid in toyland at Christmastime.

So far I had drunk only beer. I was getting higher and higher and didn't know it. After a while, they ran out of beer and I found a bottle of Canadian Club in a kitchen cabinet with a shot glass next to it. I was with a girl, so I poured her a shot, then took one myself. I'm unsure about what happened after that, except to say that I finished the bottle. After that, Tony Horton told me he saw me leave the place with two girls, one on each arm.

About five or six the next morning, Tony got a call in his room at the Commodore. The two girls had called him to tell him to come down to Greenwich Village right away and take me back. Tony and Mike Ryan came downtown in a cab and found me, rolling around drunk on the floor. I didn't have all my clothes on, I was told later, and I certainly didn't know who Tony and Mike were.

They had paid a cab driver $5 to wait for them, and after they got me dressed they took me back to the Commodore. I was throwing up and my head was spinning. Somehow, they got me back to the room without being discovered and tried sobering me up. I was as sick as a dog, and after a while, I fell asleep.

I was in worse shape when I got up. I couldn't look at my breakfast, much less eat it, and I barely could walk a straight line. When it came time to get on the bus, I was sick all over again and took a seat next to the window. One of the sports-writers sat down next to me and began reading a newspaper. As the bus started, I felt nauseated and knew I needed air in a hurry. I slid the window open and stuck my head out, but all I got was the bus fumes. I pulled back in and suddenly heaved everything right in the lap of the writer next to me. We were both a mess.

When we got to Yankee Stadium Mike Ryan stayed behind with me till everybody else was off the bus, then he helped me get down to the locker room. I headed right for the john where I continued to throw up for several more minutes. Never again, I promised myself. Jack Fadden came back to give me something to soothe my stomach, and then somebody came and told me Billy Herman wanted to see me in his office right away.

If anything will sober you up, a command like that will. I tucked in my shirt and went to see him. Herman slammed the door shut behind us and said, "You're drunk."

"No I'm not," I said. "I'm just a little sick to my stomach."

"Well, I say you're drunk," Herman said, "but this will make you sick. This is going to cost you $1,000." I knew he was mad because his face was real red and his fists were clenched. But $1,000 was a lot of money.

"I'm all right, really," I kept insisting. "I am not drunk."

"Well, if you're not drunk," Herman said, "you're gonna play right field today. How's that?"

Like a fool I said okay. I don't know how I got through that game. Practically every inning I puked into my glove, though by this time I was dry-heaving more than anything else. On top of that, Mel Stottlemyre was pitching. I managed to walk once and strike out once, and then in the eighth inning, I came up with the tie-breaking run on third base. When Stottlemyre pitched I saw three baseballs coming in at me; luckily I picked out the right one because I hit a short fly ball to the outfield. It wasn't terribly deep, but the runner on third was alert, and as soon as the catch was made he dashed home with the winning run.

When the team got back to Boston, my father called me at my apartment. "Come on over here right away," he said to me.

"Why?" I asked. "What's up?"

"We are going down to the Red Sox office and get this whole mess straightened out," he said. "It's gone too far already."

When I got to the house we got in my father's car and drove to town. My father told me he had called Neil Mahoney that morning and insisted on a private meeting right away to clear the air. He told me that Mike Higgins and Billy Herman would be there, too. Then he said, "And keep your mouth shut unless I tell you to say something. Understand?" I nodded my head yes.

We got to the office around noon. They were all there waiting for us. My father did a lot of the talking when we sat down. He said to Herman, "In Cleveland, Tony was out after hours. Right?"

"That's right," Herman said.

"How late? Twenty minutes?"

"More like forty minutes," Herman said.

"All right, forty minutes then," my father said. "Did you tell Tony to deny he was out late if the writers asked him about it?"

"Well, yes," Herman said.

"Then why the hell didn't you protect the kid when they jumped all over him?" my father asked.

"Well, I have twenty-four other ballplayers to worry about," Herman said.

"We're not here to discuss twenty-four other ballplayers. We're here because Tony is going crazy and he can't hit with these things bothering him. Now, look. We'll apologize. Tony was wrong, but I want this thing ended right here in this office now. For crying out loud, what was so bad about being forty minutes late? You're his boss. Why didn't you just tell him to take it like a man and let it go at that? Wouldn't that have been a lot better than all this lying stuff?"

After that, everyone agreed on making a press release explaining we had all talked it out and the problem had been solved. My father helped to write it and when it was finished copies were handed out to the writers who were hovering around outside. One of them came up to my father and said, "What's up?"

My father said, "Did you see the release?"

The guy said yes he did.

"Well, what more can I tell you?" he said. He was hot, but still in control.

Later on I got a call from Tom Yawkey's secretary telling me he would like to see me. She told me he'd meet me in the stands at

Fenway Park the next day. It was well before the start of a night game, so when I arrived he and I were the only two people there. He asked me about New York and I told him the whole story. When I was through he said to me, "Tell me, was it worth it?"

I thought I knew what he was asking and I laughed. "Believe me, Mr. Yawkey," I said, "I was so drunk and so sick, I don't even remember." He laughed and then told me to forget the past and just go out there and "knock the cover off the ball." That's the kind of man he is, and I knew I'd hustle for his ballclub as long as I played for it.

After that, I went off on a pretty good hitting streak. For the next week I batted at a .453 clip that included five more homers. Then, on July 28, it happened all over again. I was hit on the right wrist by a pitch thrown by Wes Stock of the Kansas City A's and had another hairline fracture. It was my fourth broken bone in three years as a pro and I missed twenty-four games.

But when I got back I continued to hit till the end of the season and I wound up winning the American League's home-run title with 32. At twenty I was the youngest player ever to do so. In addition, I batted .269 and knocked in 82 runs, 30 more than I did in my rookie year. I hit my thirty-second homer on the last day of the season. I also happened to drop a fly ball during the game. So leave it to Roger Birtwell of the *Globe* to end my season on the right note. His story the next day was headlined: "Tony C. Drops Fly Ball." I was mad, but by the time I saw the piece I was on a rickety train headed for Fort Dix, New Jersey, for six months of Army Reserve duty.

In 1966 I managed to avoid any serious injuries for the first time and I had a good year. I batted .265 and collected 28 homers and 93 RBI's and was named the Red Sox' Most Valuable Player. But the team finished ninth for the second year in a row and Herman was fired. I can't say I was sorry. We never had any more trouble after that meeting, but we still never got along. I have never seen a manager like Herman. I think he cared more about the newspapermen than he did about his own ballplayers. He was always sitting with the writers from town to town—all the players on the club noticed this. He wasn't a manager who protected his players, which is the type of manager I like

The man who replaced Herman in 1967 was Dick Williams. You've got to say he did an incredible job, taking a ballclub that finished ninth two years straight and managing it to a pennant. If Williams ever was likable it was in 1967. That's because we were up there fighting for something, and personalities never came up. We were a happy ballclub and showed up every day knowing we were going to win.

One day during that season Ed Penney, who was then my business manager, said to me, "By the way, I saw Ted Williams recently and he told me to tell you to stop crowding the plate. He said you should get back before one of those guys hits you."

I was in a slight slump at the time and I said, "Who'd want to hit me the way I'm hitting?"

The date was August 18, 1967.

PART III

When I hit that home run on opening day 1969 in Baltimore, the cheering of the crowd, the back-slapping of my teammates and the pure joy I felt in my heart should have been the whole story. I was still in the big leagues; I had hit a home run; I was back where I had started before Jack Hamilton's pitch nearly killed me. Everybody believed it. Well, that just wasn't so. I was far from being back, and I was the only one in the world who knew it.

I couldn't blame anybody for thinking so. I helped it along by telling the writers how I could see everything perfectly, but it wasn't the whole truth. All the accounts of my last eye examination reported that my sight had completely returned; and in truth, the doctors at the Retina Associates stated in a release that my left eye had returned to 20/20-1, meaning I could. read the 20-line with the exception of one letter. Technically, that was so; actually, it wasn't.

With the exception of the people I feel especially close to—my parents and brothers, Joe Tauro, my roommate Tony Athanas, Jr., Uncle Vinnie, Dr. Regan, Jack Zanger—I have never before told anyone that my eye is far from being perfect. Today, if I close my good eye and stare out at the pitcher holding a baseball in his hand, I still have difficulties. If I'm looking straight at the pitcher's hand, I see no hand and no ball in it. But if I look approximately a foot to the left of what I want to see, my peripheral vision (which was not damaged in the beaning) enables me to pick out the hand and the ball. That's the same way I read the eye chart in Dr. Regan's office. If I stared directly at the chart with my left eye only, all I could see was the big E on top. But when I looked a couple of inches to the left, I could read all the way down to the 20-line, with the exception of one letter.

My friends have asked me why I'm willing to reveal this now that I am back in baseball and hitting; won't the pitchers I face be able to take advantage of me knowing about this deficiency? My answer to that is they can't bear down on me any harder now than they've done so many times in the past—before my beaning and after it. I have enough broken bones to prove that. But I always knew way down inside myself that if I ever did make it back it would have to be with one eye. Another reason I'm admitting it: I'm proud that I did come back.

Sure, I can see the ball coming in better now because my left eye improved well enough to work with my right eye in what they call binocular vision. But when both my eyes are open watching a baseball coming at me at ninety miles an hour, I can't tell my left eye to look a foot to the left to pick it out. So I know that what I did last year I did with my right eye. Because the left eye improved the way it did I was able to see the ball and the way it broke. But if anyone knew last year that I was having this difficulty, I never would have made it back, because the first time

I went into a slump they'd say, "Well, there it is. He's really blind in the eye and can't see." Do you think I would have been given another chance? So I think I proved something last year, to myself and to everybody else.

After my tenth-inning homer in the opener put us ahead, Frank Robinson came up in the bottom of the tenth and hit a homer to make it 4–4. The game was still going in the twelfth when I led off. Mike Adamson, a big right-hander, was on the mound for Baltimore. I saw he could throw hard. He threw a curve up around the shoulders and I swung and missed. He threw another in the same spot and I swung and missed again. Then he threw me two balls. On the 2–2 pitch he threw me a fastball at the knees. It looked just a little low to me and I let it go by. I was right. Finally, I took one high for ball four. To the Red Sox it was the potential tie-breaking run; to me it meant I was correctly judging pitches again. We loaded the bases and then Dalton Jones hit one deep to right and I scored easily from third. We won the game, 5–4.

The minute the game was over, Fitzy came running into the dugout to tell me to stay there; Ned Martin was going to interview me for TV. I sat and waited and when we went on the air I told them that I had just hoped to have a respectable day and that I was naturally happy to have hit the home run when I did. But I told him the best part was winning, and I meant it.

When I got back to the clubhouse, the guys began coming around in droves. "Way to go, C.," said Reggie Smith. "Just like old times again." The writers were there, too, and I told them it had been a long time between my 104th home run and my 105th. But I also said that for me the season wouldn't be officially opened till we got back to Boston. All through the months and weeks of my comeback, I had been telling myself that I was doing this for my own fans, the ones who'd been writing me and praying for me all this time, and whom I knew would be there when I came back.

We lost the next game to the Orioles, again in extra innings, and then off for Cleveland where we had a three-game weekend series before heading home for Boston. For the third straight game, we played extra innings and won this one in the sixteenth, 2–1. But in the thirteenth inning I came face to face with my past. Jack Hamilton was with the Indians now and had come in to pitch. This was the first time I had seen him since that night in 1967, and when I stepped in I don't know how I didn't crack my teeth, I wanted to get a hit so badly.

As I dug in, I told myself to get even a little closer to the plate than I'd been standing. I wanted to prove I wasn't afraid of him. We had a guy on base, and when I looked down to Pop at third base, he flashed me the bunt sign. I wanted to scream something out, but I didn't; I laid one down and the runner moved up. Hamilton was still in there when I came up the next time. I have rarely wanted a hit so badly in my life, and never for such a personal reason. I leaned over the plate and when I saw the one I liked I really laid into it, sending a deep line drive to left field that Lee Maye caught. I had hit the ball right on the button; I couldn't hit a ball any harder.

After the game the writers came over to my locker to ask me about Hamilton. I didn't want to tell them anything. "He's just the same as any other pitcher to me," I told them. "No, there wasn't any funny feeling when I saw him out there." I wanted to bury the subject. To this day Hamilton and I haven't said anything to each other, not that we ever did before the beaning. I know it was an accident, but I honestly don't know if I have ever really forgiven him for it.

On Sunday we flew back to Boston. My whole family was at Logan Airport to greet Billy and me—my parents, Richie, Uncle Vinnie and Aunt Phyllis, and my uncles Joe and Guy. The moment I saw my father's face the thought that crossed my mind was what was he thinking now, seeing both Billy and me coming off that plane together. He had spent his whole life for us, and now not one, but two of his sons were with the Red Sox. I hoped he was as proud of us and the job he had done as I was of him at that moment.

We all went back to the house, where my mother cooked supper for everybody. This is when she's the happiest, spooning out those great things from her pots. She made gnocchi—her specialty —which is a mixture of homemade macaroni and potatoes, along with veal Parmesan, chicken cacciatore, her special chicken soup, artichokes, stuffed peppers, and stuffed macaroni. In our house the food keeps coming. The funny thing is my father, my brothers, and I are all pretty lean, but my mother, who never sits down, is always complaining, "You'd think I'd lose weight that way." We don't usually have much room for dessert after one of her meals, but a couple of hours later she'll bring around the ice cream and strawberry shortcake.

Afterwards, a lot of neighbors dropped in and we had a great time. Just before going up to bed, I told my father, "Tomorrow is going to be the biggest day of my life." Then I lay awake unable to fall asleep. If anything, this was even worse than that first night in Baltimore.

The next morning Billy and I left early for the ballpark. The folks would come out later. When I got to Fenway, I put on a golf hat and sunglasses so I wouldn't be recognized. I knew there'd be a lot of people who would know me and come up to wish me good luck, and I was trying to cut down on the number.

Our clubhouse was alive with nervous people. The radio was blaring when I walked in and the guys were pacing, clapping each other on the back and shaking hands quietly. It's always this way at the start of a season. My locker was now against a wall at the extreme end of the clubhouse, about as far away from the manager's office as it could be without being outside. I was there with my brother Billy, Rico, and George Scott. "I see they put all the Italians together," I cracked and Scotty grinned.

I tried to dress as quickly as I could and get out on the field. I had been away for a long time. A few writers were there and they came over to wish me luck. They seemed to have the good sense to make it very brief. I was getting very up tight about this game. Finally, I was ready and headed for the door. I went down the stairs, into a darkened runway, and finally into the dugout itself. From where I looked up, I saw blue skies. As I got to the top step of the dugout, I very deliberately flipped my glove out on the field. I was back.

Nobody was there yet. For a moment I was alone, just the way I had been when I came to work out in front of the empty stands with Moe. I knew what today was. I knew it all through me, right down to my stomach which was quaking like Jello. I ran into the outfield and jogged for a while, trying to calm myself down, reminding myself I still had a long way to go. I was so high and yet so sick, I was afraid I wasn't going to live long enough to make the game.

When I came back to the dugout, I could see the fans trickling into the stands, and some of the guys had come out and were throwing a ball around. I reached for my glove where I had tossed it, and somebody told me my grandfather was up in the stands. I went up there and I kissed him. He's my mother's father and is eighty-two years old.

During batting practice I was still so tight I felt I wasn't going to make the next breath. I then tried kidding myself out of it. Harrelson was waiting his turn nearby and I said, "The first thing they gotta do around here is cut the grass, right? It's much too long." He turned and smiled at me, but I guess he had something on his mind, too. I took cuts and felt like I was going to throw up. So I went over to Pop and told him, "I can't take infield today. I'm sick to my stomach."

"Sure," he said. "All right, I'll tell Dick. Look, go on downstairs to the clubhouse and rest till it's time, all right?" I nodded, went back to the trainer's room and sprawled on a table. My mind was fuzzy and my stomach was quivering. I just lay there staring upwards and wondering if it was all a dream.

The stands were buzzing when I got back to the dugout. Ken Coleman, who broadcasts the Red Sox games, was at the mike at home plate and he was just beginning to introduce the Orioles. He began with their manager, Earl Weaver, then the coaches, then all the players, starting with the lowest number and working up. Then he got to us. There was Williams and Pop and Bobby Doerr and Darrell Johnson; then he started with No. 2, Mike Andrews. All our guys got big ovations, of course. Then Coleman way saying, No. 24, Juan Pizarro, and Juan ran onto the field. Before Coleman could even begin my number, a roar began in the stands, and Coleman quickly said, No. 25 . . . but he never got to say my name, or if he did, nobody heard him.

I raced onto the field and the crowd got up. I was grinning and shivering at the same time. I stood there next to Pizarro and listened to the beautiful sound coming from all those people. First I waved, but when they wouldn't stop, I pulled off my cap and waved it over my head, trying to look in every direction at the same time. It must have lasted about two minutes; I felt proud.

It was great while it lasted, but I felt a lot better when it stopped and I knew I had cleared another hurdle.

The game finally started. When I came up in the first inning, we already had scored a run, Yaz was on second, Harrelson on first, and there was one out. But just as soon as I stepped in, the crowd started all over again, this time even louder than before. I could see Mike Cuellar wasn't going to pitch and the umpire said to me, "Maybe you better step out and let them get it out of their systems." I stood there staring down now because my eyes were filling up with tears and I was wondering to myself how I could hit and cry at the same time. *Relax,* I told myself. *Relax and sit back.*

But I couldn't relax. Cuellar threw me a screwball and I went after it in too much of a hurry and missed. I saw the ball all right, but my swing was awful. He threw me another screwball and I did the same thing. Damn. I was mad at myself. *You're over-anxious,* I told myself. The next one was where I expected it, on the outside, and I let it go for a ball. Then he threw me a fastball outside and I sliced it out to right field where Frank Robinson caught it. Yaz tagged up after the catch and went to third. But we had to settle for one run.

We were leading, 2–0, when I came up again in the third. Yaz had led off with a double and gone to third after Harrelson lined out to Robinson in right. As I walked up to the plate, the crowd started in again. Only this time it was different. They had welcomed me back the first time. Now they were saying, "Come on, Tony, knock that run in." Again, Cuellar got me to swing and miss on his first two pitches. I then shortened up on the bat and hit the next ball hard but right at the shortstop, Mark Belanger. The infield was drawn in and Belanger fired the ball home and they trapped Yaz in a rundown play. Yaz jockeyed back and forth long enough for me to race to second base. Boomer then ripped a single to center and I came home with the run.

An inning later, though, it was a new ballgame as the Orioles tied the score at 3–3. When I got up again in the bottom of the fourth inning, we had loaded the bases with one out. If I'd had any doubts before that the crowd was with me, they were dispelled now. Whatever nervousness I had felt before was all gone now. I was glad to be coming up in a spot like this because I knew if I could get a hit I'd be doing it for these great people.

The Orioles had brought in the kid right-hander I'd seen on opening day down there, Mike Adamson. His first pitch sailed right at the point of my chin. I pulled only my head back and I could hear the crowd gasp like one man. The pitch really didn't bother me: nobody brushes you back deliberately in a spot like that, bases loaded, tie-breaking run on third. Earl Weaver confirmed this when he ran out of the dugout and said something to Adamson. I read the next day that he wanted Adamson to pitch me low and away and the first one had slipped off his fingers. Adamson came back with a good fastball and I swung at it as hard as I could. I got only a small piece of the ball and topped it toward third base. Great Brooks Robinson plays there, only the best. I took off as fast as I could. My legs ran ahead of my body. Digging as hard as I could, I got to the bag just a fraction before I heard the ball crash into Boog Powell's mitt. Mike Andrews scored from third base for us, and as things turned out my fifteen-foot hit knocked in the winning run of the game.

It didn't matter to me how far the ball went. "Hell, I'll take eighty more of those if they'll win ballgames for us," I told the writers crowded around my locker afterwards. "If it had been anyone else but Brooks, I could have jogged down to first." The writers kept asking questions, about the eye, how it felt to get the winning hit, and again and again the flash bulbs were popping. "Imagine getting all this ink for a fifteen-foot hit," I said.

But I wasn't being flip. It had been quite a day. During the game while I stood in right field, a kid jumped out of the stands and came running over to shake my hand. The crowd got a kick out of it, and so did I. The kid said to me, "You're the only reason I'm here." And I said to the kid, "Well you won't be for long; here come the cops." They came and got him and believe it or not, the fans booed.

I had wanted so badly to do something good on this first day. These people were swinging the bat for me. That same morning I got a letter from a nun in Rome who said she was having a mass said for me and she prayed that I would win the opening game for the Red Sox. Unbelievable, isn't it? God works in strange ways. Like that fifteen-foot game-winning hit.

A couple of days later I had to sit out a game because of a stiff knee, and Williams decided to use Billy in my place. It was the right move since the Orioles were starting a left-hander, Dave McNally, and Billy batted from the right side. I'm sure he would have gone with Joe Lahoud, who hits lefty, if they pitched a right-hander. Although Billy had played a few games in the majors, this was his first start—and in Boston, yet. So I knew how he felt. He struck out in his first at-bat. But his next time up Billy hit a home run against Dave Leonhard. The whole bench was waiting for him when he got back. I knew how happy he was, but he was trying not to show it. I was crazy with joy. Then, in true Conigliaro fashion, he hit another homer his next time up. He looked a lot more relaxed after this one. Sticking to the family tradition, when Billy came up for his last at-bat, he struck out.

"I guess I better go to Pittsfield and learn how to play another position," I kidded Billy in the clubhouse afterward. Billy laughed, but when the writers came around he wouldn't let them get him to say anything even jokingly about his taking my place. "Tony is our rightfielder," he told them. "No one is going to take his job. I'm just glad I was able to get a few hits." I was proud of him—both for his two homers and for saying what he did. I'm glad they gave him the ink the next day; he deserved it. I couldn't play the next day, either, and Billy had another big game, getting his third homer, a single and a double. Funny how much better my knee felt the next day.

The Indians came to town and I belted my second homer of the year, as we won, 10–7. At this point, I was feeling good and seeing the ball good. Not great, but I was able to follow it all the way in. Up to now, things with Dick Williams were peaceful. We both kept our distance. The writers were nice and the fans were pulling for me on every pitch. These things weren't made to last.

Things began innocently enough when the Red Sox traded Harrelson (along with Juan Pizarro and Dick Ellsworth) to the Indians on April 19. In return we got Sonny Siebert, Vicente Romo, and Joe Azcue. The Red Sox probably figured I was back and what they now needed more than power was pitching. Harrelson had been our cleanup hitter, and now with him gone, I hoped Williams would put me there. That's where I feel I have always been at my best, where I could drive in runs. But he kept me batting sixth and sometimes fifth for the next several games. When the Yankees came to Fenway, I hit a three-run homer that beat them, and got three hits and my fourth homer the next day against the Senators. I was hitting an even .300 and leading the ballclub in game-winning hits.

Finally, when we went to Detroit Williams put me in the fourth slot. On Saturday our game was seen nationally as part of NBC's

Game of the Week. Bill Rigney, then managing the California Angels, saw the game and was later quoted as saying, "Conigliaro is not quite as ready as we had been led to believe. He's bailing out and that's something he never did before."

Maybe I shouldn't have gotten so steamed up about it, but after all that hard work I thought it was an unnecessary crack. But I told myself, "For once in your life keep quiet about it. Just wait till we get out there the first time and I'll make him eat his words."

Then we came to New York and more trouble, but not with the Yankees. On the first night, my old friend Merv Griffin came to see the game and brought along his young son, Tony. After the game, Merv took Billy and me out to dinner and we met comedian Jack E. Leonard there. He did a job on me. "Who the hell ever heard of the Capistrano brothers?" he roared at Billy and me.

The next afternoon, I was resting in my room when my phone rang. It was Merv. "Come on over to the studio for a couple of minutes," he said. "I want you to meet somebody."

"Who?" I asked.

"Never mind," he said. "Just come on over."

I knew it had to be a girl, so I dressed quickly and went over. His show was rehearsing and when Merv spotted me he jogged over just the way he does on camera. "How's your hitting?" I kidded him.

He laughed. "Just fine," he said. "By the way, how's yours?" I laughed and said, "It could always be better."

While we stood there I heard a female voice going over a song. I looked up and there was Mamie Van Doren. Sure, I recognized her right away. Wouldn't you? Merv and I moved up front and took seats. When she was finished Merv called her over and introduced us. The first thing that amazed me about her—after I got over the way she looked, of course—was that she knew all about me, the Red Sox, and my accident. We hit it off right away and I asked her to go out with me after the game that night. She said fine.

Just before I left Merv offered me the use of his limousine. "You might as well go in style," he told me. I told him I wouldn't need it because *Sports Illustrated* was going to pick up Billy and me after the game and drive us to a photo studio so they could shoot some pictures of us. It was supposed to be for a cover. So Merv kept his limousine and it was arranged that it would take Mamie to the studio later on.

We won the game, 2–1, coming from behind to give Mel Stottlemyre his first defeat of the season. The Red Sox were trailing, 1–0, when I doubled in the seventh and scored on a single by Syd O'Brien. He later scored on a wild throw. After the game Billy and I were taken downtown for a couple of hours of shooting. While we were there Merv's limousine picked up Mamie and brought her over and she watched. After a while the photographer took some photos of Mamie and me, and the more he shot the less he was interested in me.

After that the three of us got in the car and I dropped Billy off someplace. Why not? He'd do the same for me, though I think Billy was kind of hoping I'd get out instead of him. Then I took Mamie to Bachelors III for dinner, and I was back in my hotel room in time for curfew. Who would think something like that would create havoc in a guy's life?

I do now. When we got back to Boston, my fan mail began to change drastically. Usually I get around 300 letters a week, a good many of them from teen-agers. Most of them are friendly, asking for an autographed photo and that's about all. But now

209

some of these kids—girls, obviously—were writing tough things like "drop dead" because I had dated Mamie. One letter even came from a ninety-five-year-old woman in Maine asking me what was I doing going out with an old hag like Mamie. I got enough mail on Mamie alone to fill the pages of this book. It was to get worse.

Against the Tigers, I doubled in the first game as we won, then dropped a squeeze bunt the next day to break up a 5–5 tie as we won again. The following day, a Sunday afternoon game, I was miserable: I struck out four times. That was also the day Dick Williams told Billy he was sending him down to Louisville. "He's hitting .317," I beefed to the writers. "Billy has worked so hard. I think it's rotten." That was also the day I noticed the background at Fenway wasn't too good. We had a packed house and for the first time that I could remember the left corner of the center-field bleachers were filled, and a lot of the people were wearing white shirts. From home plate, this section was behind the pitcher, and it was hard to see the pitched ball. I guess when I complained about it afterwards, I sounded like a crybaby.

But the truth of the matter is I didn't ever remember hitting against that kind of background before. When I was hurt in 1967, we weren't drawing that well and those seats were not sold. It was only after the Red Sox made their pennant run that bigger crowds began showing up, so those seats were filled. In that Sunday game against the Tigers, I remember standing at the plate and actually being frightened like I was at Pompano Beach in 1968 when I couldn't see anything they were throwing. *Someone is going to get killed,* I told myself. *I can't even see curve balls.* So I popped off after the game and got myself into a brand-new stew with the ballclub, which I needed like another hole in my eye.

"We will continue to use those seats when the public wants them," said Dick O'Connell.

"I won't play unless something is done about it," I said. My timing was bad, as usual. We were leaving the next day for our first trip to the West Coast, so by the time we had left I had stirred a lot of people up, but that was about all.

Our first stop was Seattle, where we won both games. My first time at bat in Seattle, I hit a line shot over the left center-field fence. After swinging I buckled over and couldn't move. I had wrenched my back painfully and was having trouble breathing. Buddy LeRoux and Dick Williams came running out. "What's wrong, kid?" asked Buddy. When I answered that I couldn't move, Dick Williams asked the umpire if he could put in a pinch runner. The umpire said yes, but the pinch runner would be credited with the home run. I looked at them and said, "Wait a minute; I'll make it around." So I started my long journey around the bases bent over double. About five minutes later, I crossed the plate and headed for the dugout. My teammates gave me a standing ovation. Dick Scofield said, "I've been around baseball a long time and thought I'd seen it all, but that move of yours belongs in Hollywood."

Then we went to Anaheim for a series against the Angels and my old pal, Bill Rigney. Anaheim is also where I saw Mamie for the second time. The papers found out about it, of course, and all the headlines on both coasts read: "Tony C. and Mamie." This was our second date, and some writers asked me if our relationship had reached the point of our being engaged. Relationship? I had seen the girl twice. I answered, "I wouldn't say so," which I thought was a pretty innocent remark, but you should have seen how that was handled in the press.

Before the start of our first game with the Angels I told a

writer that I planned on hitting a home run that night. "I plan to dedicate it to Bill Rigney," I told him. What he had said a couple of weeks earlier continued to bug me and I wanted him to eat his words. In the first inning I singled against Andy Messersmith. Now I was up again in the third and there was no score. Yaz was on base. Messersmith fired one and I cracked it on a towering shot to deepest left. I could see Rick Reichardt going all the way back for it, then reaching up for the ball. It struck his glove, then trickled over the fence by the Angel bullpen. I deliberately broke into a slow trot going around the bases and when I rounded third base I just glared into the Angel dugout at Rigney. But that was all. When the writers came around after the game I refused to say anything more about it. We had won the game, 7–2, and I was now hitting .300. I wanted to let it go at that.

The next night the game was tied at 3–3 after nine innings. In the tenth I came up with the bases loaded against Ricky Clark and lined one to deep center. Nobody was going to catch this one, and while the three runners scored ahead of me, I made it into third with a triple. That gave us a 6–3 win. Out in right field after I'd hit my triple, some kids who'd been waving a flag that said "Conig" waved it wildly. I had now hit safely in nine of my last ten games, collecting 14 hits, boosted my average to .305, and had 5 homers and 21 RBI's. The following day we completed a sweep of the Angels as Rico, with a sick stomach, homered twice. We had now won eight games in a row.

The Oakland Athletics ended our streak, but we came back to win the next night. What a great trip this had been. We'd won seven out of eight in the West and were going home in second place just three and a half games behind the Orioles. I got 3 hits against Oakland, giving me 9-for-29 on the trip for a .310 average.

I had knocked in 10 runs and hit a homer. I felt great; my confidence was growing and I felt strong. Little did I suspect that back home in Boston a new revolution was brewing.

First, the Mamie business was being played well out of proportion. All the writers had a shot at me for that, my fan mail from teen-age kids was bitter, and my parents didn't like it, either. I had a date with a well-known and sexy actress and no matter what I say about it the writers interpret it any way they want. Just as long as it makes good copy. One writer asked me how serious I was about Mamie and I told him I wasn't going to go out with her again for a long time. He chuckled and asked me what I meant by a long time, so I kidded him back and said, "About a day." That's the way he printed it, and nobody called attention to the fact that Mamie had already left for South America.

Then there was the white-shirt incident. As soon as I got back to Boston I heard that the Red Sox had solved the problem of those bleacher seats. On days they knew they were going to have a full house they would make those 900 seats available but ask the fans who were going to sit out there to wear dark clothing. I felt that was a fair-enough compromise; after all, 900 seats in a ballpark with only 33,375, represents a sizable loss if they can't use them. But to ease things, the club printed up little cards which they handed out to everybody who sat out there.

The cards read: "You are now an official member of Conig's Corner. The Red Sox and Tony C. appreciate your cooperation in helping to provide a good hitting background," and they were signed, "The Boston Red Sox."

I didn't like the idea of identifying the problem as Conig's Corner. Sure, I was the guy who had spoken up for what I thought was a legitimate problem. I didn't want to go up there facing the pitcher against that blanket of white shirts. But why Conig's Corner? Every hitter in the league benefited by it, and several Red Sox players told me they were glad something finally had been done about it. Somebody even went so far as to tell me the reason the Red Sox finally gave in was because I was leading the club in runs-batted-in at the time.

So what happened in my first game back under the new rule? I had my worst game of the season. I went 0-for-5, striking out 4 times and banging into a double play, and to top things off, we lost the ballgame in 11 innings, 10–9.

It really wasn't anything new. All my life I seem to have had the bad luck—or maybe bad judgment—to say something I shouldn't have, or I've not said something when I should have. I'm not sorry I spoke up about those white shirts, but maybe I could have handled it a little better. As for the 0-for-5 against Seattle, while I have no excuse, I didn't tell anybody that I spent my first day back in Boston getting another Army physical. I was in the Reserve, and after all my trouble with the eye over the two previous years they wanted to test me themselves to see what my status was. So I went down there at 11 A.M., they dilated my eye, and I didn't get away till just before game time that night. I didn't tell anybody where I'd been all day and I played the game. I know I was tired and worn out from a whole day of having my eye picked at all over again. I probably should have done the smart thing and gone to Williams and told him I could use the night off.

In the next game I struck out three times. I went into a bad slump, during which my average dipped to .279, striking out 12 times in 20 at-bats and getting only one hit in 14 times up. Williams came over to me and said, "I'm going to move you down to the sixth spot in the batting order to take some of the pressure off you."

"I don't want to bat sixth," I told him. "I want to bat fourth. There's not that much pressure."

But he said, "We'll just move you down for a few days, then we'll move you back later on."

I didn't like it. I felt I had been doing a good job up to then and didn't deserve being moved down because of a slump. I'd hit my way out of it, I knew I would. But Williams was the manager and he called the shots. From that day on, I began to lose my confidence. I didn't feel the same anymore. Maybe I should have known better, but who had time to think clearly? I took the whole thing as a demotion.

Now the pressures really began to close in on me. My slump helped bring out the worst in the Boston writers. They were sure it had to be Mamie's fault. Nobody considered the fact that my slump began about ten days after I had last seen her in Anaheim— or that I was busting the ball out on the Coast when I did see her. It was much easier to blame it on her. That bothered me, because she really is a nice girl, and I told one writer I'd go out with her if she was eighty years old. But standing out in right field at Fenway I'd hear things like, "Mamie's too much for you Tony."

What hurt was that most of it came from teen-age kids. I never realized what an impact a thing like this would have. I got these letters every day, one from a girl telling me she saw me play in Cleveland and wants to marry me; but now that I was planning on marrying a thirty-six-year-old woman she was absolutely fractured and might even kill herself. They were very sad letters, and what they were saying to me was that they didn't want me to get married. Well, I wasn't getting married. I was doing what I wanted to do, but when that doesn't fit the picture your so-called fans have of you, they turn against you.

The writers helped out a lot. I was in a slump, and they said, it was Mamie's fault. Bunk. I was in a slump, that's all. Lots of ballplayers have slumps, but not all of them have dates with Mamie Van Doren, which is what I think it was all about in the first place. I'm single and I like girls. I do something about it, so that makes me easy prey, especially in a town like Boston where some of the writers think ballplayers should be saints.

So I really was down now. The Boston fans were booing me. I didn't know if it was because of Mamie, my slump, or both. Dick Williams wasn't talking to me. He had dropped me to the sixth slot. The writers were printing their theories about Mamie and me. My fan mail had turned to hate mail. On top of that, I really wasn't sure about my comeback. Was I seeing the ball well enough? I really didn't know then. But the worst of it was the booing at Fenway. These were the fans I had told myself I was coming back for, and every time I struck out now, I'd hear things like, "Get your rest, Tony. Leave Mamie alone."

I needed the fans. More than anyone else I needed the fans. I knew my teammates were with me. They were always slapping me on the back, telling me how good I looked at the plate. I needed encouragement very much. But when the fans began to turn against me, I really wondered if it was worth the struggle to come back. I'd strike out and I'd hear things like, "Go home, blind man," or "Get Lahoud in there," and at times, "We want Billy." Lovely things.

Sometimes I'd stand there for a moment at the plate silently saying to them, "If you knew the truth you wouldn't boo. I'm trying very hard and I need your help. You all think my eye is perfect again, just like before. Well, you're wrong." It got so bad I hated going to the ballpark anymore. Everyone and everything was bugging me now. I'd leave the ballpark wearing a floppy golf hat and sunglasses and sneak out different exits so I wouldn't be recognized. I never thought I'd feel that way again, but now I did.

By the end of May, though, my slump was over. My average began to climb again. On May 31, I knocked in the winning run in a 3–2 game over the Twins. The next day I went 4-for-4 and hit a homer, as Rico and I knocked in all our runs in a 5–2 win over the Senators. My average was back to .288. I had 10 homers and was leading the club with 37 RBI's. Still, Williams batted me sixth.

June was a miserable month for us. The club went into a tailspin. Jim Lonborg broke a toe. Jose Santiago still couldn't pitch after off-season arm surgery. Mike Andrews was out of the lineup for five weeks. George Thomas was out for the season, Joe Azcue, the catcher we had got from the Indians, jumped the club in Kansas City because he felt Williams wasn't playing him enough, and he had to be traded to the Angels for Tom Satriano. I like Tom, but a lot of the guys on the ballclub thought Azcue could have meant the pennant to us if Williams had handled him differently. A lot of writers even said so in print, and these were the same guys who were drinking buddies of Williams.

After the Azcue incident we seemed to lose our incentive. There are things a manager can do to shake a ballclub up when something like this happens. Maybe Williams could have changed his ways, talked to somebody, even if not to me. But he was locked in, as stubborn as he had always been. He didn't talk to anybody. He just walked through our clubhouse, head down, going about his business, but having nothing or very little to say to any of us. We were not what you would call a happy ballclub.

Williams' style is illustrated by what he did to me one afternoon in the middle of June. We were getting beaten bad by Oakland when, about halfway through the game, Williams came out to make another pitching change. I wandered over toward Reggie Smith for a little conversation, when I saw Joe Lahoud coming my way. At first I figured he was going out to our bullpen for something. But he came up to me and said, "I'm in for you." Lahoud couldn't have shocked me any more if he had struck me in the face.

I walked slowly toward our dugout with my head down. My blood was boiling. When I got to the dugout I looked for Williams, figuring maybe he'd explain this move to me. But his back was turned. So I headed down the stairs for the clubhouse. *What's he trying to do to me?* I asked myself. *He's trying to destroy me, that's what he's trying to do.*

Williams never did tell me why he took me out, but after I cooled off the best I could make of it was that he wanted to save pitchers. When Lahoud came in, he went into the pitcher's spot, while the new pitcher Williams had brought in then went into my spot. Managers are supposed to play to win no matter what the score is. I'd have given Williams that, but at least he could have taken a few minutes to tell me about it.

After that game we flew to Cleveland. On the plane, Fred Ciampa of the *Record American,* one of the Boston writers I like and trust, came over to me and said, "I guess you know you're not playing tomorrow night."

"No," I said dismally, "I didn't know. How do you know?"

"Williams just told me," Ciampa said.

That was another typical move of Williams. He'd tell the writers before he'd even think of telling one of his ballplayers. It's a matter of courtesy, not a matter of showing how tough you can be. I don't think there's a tougher manager around than

Ralph Houk of the Yankees. But his players have told me he lets them know where they stand, he talks to them. That's all I ever wanted from a manager, and Williams never gave it to me. Two games later he had me back in right field.

At the end of June we went to Washington, where we lost three out of four games. We were a dead club. The worst of it happened when we dropped a Sunday doubleheader. We blew the first game when the Senators scored three runs in the bottom of the ninth. They had a man on first in the ninth when somebody hit a fly ball to me. I came up for it, lost the ball, and it dropped in for a hit. After that, our pitcher threw away a sacrifice bunt to let one run score, another run came in on a sacrifice fly to tie the score. Then with the bases loaded and one man out, Del Unser hit a ground ball to Rico at short. A double play and we'd have extra innings. Rico fired home to Satriano for a force; then Satriano fired to first and threw the ball away. The winning run crossed the plate.

Williams was in a red rage when we got back to the clubhouse. He had a right to be. We had no business handing them that ballgame. Then I saw my name wasn't in the starting lineup for the second game. He was starting Lahoud. This had happened to me before, so I just shrugged it off as another of his piques. But after we had dropped the second game, 11–4, Williams told the writers that it was my fault we had lost the opener. "He quit on that ball," Williams said. "He cost us the game."

One of the writers pointed out that the winning run came home on Satriano's wild peg. "If Conigliaro had caught that routine fly ball, the other plays never would have come up," Williams said. This time I kept my mouth shut, angry as I was. I wasn't going to do anybody any good at a time like that by sounding off.

There is nothing more hateful to me than to be blamed for

quitting. I have never quit on anything in my life in baseball. Okay, I'll take that back. Once, earlier last year, I hit a pop fly toward the right side. The second-baseman lost the ball in the sun and it dropped untouched fifteen feet away. Henry McKenna, who was the official scorer, ruled it an error. Later in the same game, Russ Gibson hit a similar fly ball and the same thing happened to it. McKenna gave Gibson a hit. I shouldn't have let it get to me, but I did. I was sick over those two calls, and I have to admit I didn't try in my next three at-bats that day. But I never quit before or after that. Maybe I misplayed that ball down in Washington, but I didn't quit. Williams has the wrong man with a charge like that.

Things didn't get any better for a while. We came home for the July 4 holiday weekend when we were scheduled to play five games against the Senators in three days. Some holiday. Boston was hot and sticky that weekend, and our baseball wasn't much better. We had lost six games in a row and the guys were down. We were only halfway through the year and few of us looked forward to the second half. The Senators beat us in the first game, 5–1. In the second game we had a shaky 4–2 lead.

When I came up in the seventh inning of the second game, it's a wonder the fans didn't come out of the stands to get me. All I had done so far in both games was strike out three times and hit into two double plays. Rico walked in front of me to load the bases with two out. When I was still in the on-deck circle I was hoping Rico would walk. Sure, I'd had a bad day and one more strikeout wouldn't make a hell of a lot of difference. But I wanted to go up there with the bases loaded and do something right.

As I headed for the plate I heard only the boos. Bob

Humphreys was on the mound for the Senators. The first two pitches were balls. Then I swung and missed at a high slider and they started booing again. I kept telling myself, *Stay in there, be quick, don't swing at another bad ball, hit the ball hard somewhere.* He threw me another high pitch up around my shoulders and I swung and missed again. I know I looked bad swinging at it. *Damn,* I said to myself. *What's the matter with me? I could have walked in a run on those two pitches if I hadn't swung.* I stepped out of the batter's box and I heard the boos louder than before. I know what they were thinking. They were thinking I was going to strike out again. I told myself to relax and hit a line drive. So I hit the next pitch for a line drive toward Frank Howard in left field. He lumbered in for the ball and barely missed making the catch. The ball went for a double and three runs scored. It was the winning hit of the game.

As I stood there at second base enjoying my moment, a strange thing happened to me. I noticed everybody was standing up and cheering. I thought to myself, what the hell are these people doing. I was so upset, I began yelling out loud, "You frontrunning sons of bitches." And I kept yelling it out. The umpire was standing there and he started yelling out the same thing. And I said to him, "Boy, they boo you when you're down, but get a hit when they want one and they're with you all over again. What kind of people are they?" And he said, "They're frontrunning sons of bitches."

Then I heard second-baseman Bernie Allen say the same thing. I looked over at him. I was taking my lead off second at this point and I could see he was trying to explain something to me, but I couldn't answer him. I knew that he was agreeing with me, but he thought I thought he was cursing me. I didn't score so when the inning was over I stopped him on the way to his dugout and I said,"Bernie, I realize you didn't say son of a bitch at me. You were saying it to them."

"Yeah," he said, "I just wanted you to realize I wasn't saying it to you."

After the next inning, when I had come back to the dugout, some of the guys like Mike Andrews and Russ Gibson, came over to say, "Nice hitting, way to go, Tony." But Dick Williams just sat there as stony as always. He didn't look at me. He just sat there down on the end of the bench and didn't say one word to me. Then in the ninth, when the Senators loaded the bases with one out and had the potential winning run at the plate, Sparky Lyle got a guy to hit into a double play. Williams never came out of the dugout to shake Sparky's hand for the save. One of the guys told me he just headed down the runway and went straight to his office. That's the kind of man we were playing for.

During the season my Uncle Vinnie told me he had just finished reading a book titled *The Impossible Dream.* It was written by a young Boston writer named Bill McSweeney. He got the title from our great pennant victory in 1967, and after I read it, I felt that the title was one of the few honest things about the book. For example, McSweeney wrote that he was after honesty, "so that those who treasure their story will also understand the past history, the weaknesses and the strengths of a team and a game. This is their story. The story of men, doing their best, or their least, for money while in pursuit of fame."

I'll buy part of that. Sure, ballplayers play baseball for fame. Throw in money, too. That's why writers write, too, isn't it? But what McSweeney neglects to mention is that some players play because they just love baseball. We play it for the challenge of being the best and we play for pride. Sure, we are paid good

222

money for this, but McSweeney never talks about the sacrifices and hell we have to go through to get to the big leagues. Not everyone who wants fame and money gets there, you know. In fact, most of them don't. But we all start out as kids thinking we'll be the one who makes it. Fame and money don't mean a thing to us when we're dreaming of making our Little League team.

So with our fame and our money we travel for seven months of the year, living out of suitcases. We get home sometimes around four or five in the morning and then have to play a game later in the day. How about scary flights in storms, or the plain ups and downs a ballplayer goes through in one season—more ups and downs, I'll bet, than most people, including sports writers, have in a lifetime. It's not just fame and money. You have to love baseball and put up with a lot of things you don't like. I happen to love baseball and, believe it or not, I would play it for nothing.

Elsewhere in his book, McSweeney says that I resented Yastrzemski both as a rival and for what McSweeney calls Carl's bad attitude. I am supposed to have said at one time or another that Yaz never seemed to care about the ballclub, that he just didn't get involved; that it was frustrating for him being on a last-place ballclub. I'd like to know where McSweeney got that information; certainly not from me.

Without trying to sound cornball about this, I have always respected and admired Carl. To this day I still get a thrill whenever I watch him swing. I think he's great, both as a ballplayer and as a team man. He feeds on winning, and when we need a big hit in a ballgame, he's the guy I want to see going up there—if it can't be me.

In 1969 Dick Williams fined him for not hustling in Oakland one day. Williams was wrong, dead wrong. Carl had his ankle taped heavily that day and I give him credit for playing in the first place. So he didn't burn himself out running down to first base and it got him his fine. When he got back to the bench Williams came walking over like he was going to tear someone's head off. He looked at Carl and said, "That's the last time you'll loaf running the bases."

Yaz looked a little embarrassed and I couldn't blame him. He said, "I was running as well as I could."

"Like hell you were," Williams said.

"I guess it's just my old age," Yaz said.

When Williams heard that he said, "That will cost you $500. Lahoud, take left field next inning."

Yaz took his glove and his cap and without saying another word went back to the clubhouse. We all looked at each other stunned, and Boomer said to me, "T.C., there goes the ballgame." I nodded. We lost.

After the ballgame, the clubhouse was dead quiet. As usual, the writers were walking around with their ears open. They had just been in Williams' office and knew about the fine to Yaz for not hustling. Several of them came over to me and asked if I thought Yaz had run well down to first base. I made no comment. I decided to keep my mouth shut, or sure as shooting, they would misquote it in the papers back home.

Then Yaz walked over and sat down between Rico and me. "What do you think?" he asked.

I told him I still couldn't believe that Williams had taken him out of the ballgame. Yaz said, "I don't mind being fined for something I do wrong. But this time I'm right. I didn't want to leave the ballgame. I might have had a shot at winning it for us."

That's the kind of guy Yaz is, and anybody who knows him,

Mr. McSweeney, knows who to believe. I just hope Yaz didn't read *The Impossible Dream*.

One day Williams sent Lahoud up to pinch-hit for me. I didn't have anything left now. I honestly felt he was trying to humiliate me, that he never once really tried to talk things over with me. I'd had it. That night, Rico and Elsie Petrocelli and Joe Tauro happened to be over at the house in Swampscott. After dinner I said to my father, "Dad, you know how much I've loved baseball all these years. The game has been fun. But now I don't love it anymore."

I could feel the room grow quiet. My mother stopped her sewing. My father just sat there listening, the way he always does when one of us has something to say. "I have plenty of reasons," I told them. "The fans are on me like never before. I think it's mostly because of Mamie Van Doren. Ever since the papers started carrying all those stories about my date with her I've been getting hate mail, from teen-age kids. I can't stand it. Dick Williams is not talking to me. He is not trying to help me. He's ruined my confidence more and more during the season, sending Lahoud in to play right field for me, today sending him in to pinch-hit for me.

"I'm straining to see the ball on every pitch, and after the games it's the same old question over and over again, 'How's the eye, Tony? How's the eye?' I'm tired. Look, I don't want to be a quitter, but I hate every part of going to that ballpark every day. If this was happening to me while I had perfect vision I wouldn't be sitting here telling you this now. But I don't see as well as people think I do. I still have difficulties. I'm not getting the push I need from the fans and maybe it's not worth the sacrifice anymore. I have made my comeback in baseball. I did what I

225

wanted to do. I prayed for 105 home runs when all I had was 104. I don't think they realize when they're booing me that I'm doing my best out there, and I know they have Mamie Van Doren on their minds. There is a lot more to life than hitting home runs."

Everyone listened till I was finished. They all could see how serious I was and how tired. "Look, Choo," my father said. "Somehow, you have got to stick out the season. Whether you want to admit it or not, the main problem with you is Dick Williams. Maybe there'll be a change. Who knows? Your whole attitude might change. I don't think now is a good time to make such a decision. Stick it out. Wait and see how you feel after the season is over. I wouldn't quit because of Dick Williams. You're going to be in this game a lot longer than he will."

All my life my father's been there when I needed him. He'd been right so often I'd be plain stupid not to take his advice. I told him, "All right." I'd stick out the season and see. I didn't honestly believe that the club would fire Williams. But I figured even if he came back and I wanted to play, I'd go to Mr. Yawkey and ask him to trade me. I didn't want to leave Boston, but I couldn't see playing again for Williams.

Now I know why August is known as the dog days. Both the Red Sox and I were miserable that month. They slipped deeper into third place and I batted .185. The only thing that kept me going was Rico. He was the new Boston Strong Boy and among the league leaders in home runs. Rico had always been there to juice me up whenever I needed it; now I felt it was my turn to keep him loose and confident.

I remember we were taking grounders together in Seattle one day and I said to him, "Kelly, how can you get down so low on the ball?" I kept calling him Kelly because he had wanted to quit

and sell Kelly's hamburgers in 1968, and with the kind of year he
was having in '69, I didn't let him up for air.

He looked at me and said, "It's my nose. I can't pull my head
up because my nose is too heavy." He paused for a second and
then said, "By the way, is my nose that big?"

"I want to keep you for a friend," I answered.

"Is it as big as Ken Harrelson's?"

"Well," I said, "Harrelson's nose sticks out more, but yours is
a lot wider."

Rico yelled over to Santiago and said, "Hey, Jose, is Harrelson's
nose bigger than mine?"

Jose yelled back, "Forget it, you both should have been peli-
cans."

I started jumping up and down and laughing. Rico said, "What
are you laughing at? Your back looks like a bar of Nestle's
Crunch." Rico was referring to the fact that with all the hot stuff
I put on my back before games I break out with a lot of pimples.
Then he started running around in circles singing, "I am an acne
pimple, as lonesome as can be."

That shut me up.

One day, it must have been at the very end of August or early
September, I suddenly had a feeling come over me. *Look, I'm
alive. I survived. I made my comeback. March, April, May, June,
July, August. That's six months. The season was practically over
and I had played in nearly all the games. I've made it. I've really
made it.* I realized for the first time how up tight I'd been all
season, afraid that maybe the pitch after this one is the one I
wouldn't see. But I'd seen them all, some better, some not so
good, but I'd seen them. And that's when I started smacking
the ball.

On August 28, I broke out of a long slump when I hit my

seventeenth home run of the year with two on and two out in the eighth inning to give the Red Sox a 9–8 victory over the Kansas City Royals. I'd hit the ball well. You know it because you can feel it way down inside you. That was the game when a bunch of kids leaped out of the stands and held the game up for about twenty minutes while they paraded around and got a lot of autographs. I was standing at my position in right field when they came up to me and I signed about a dozen or so. Then Dick O'Connell phoned down to the dugout and told Williams to order me to stop. What could I do? I know I'm not supposed to do it, but I didn't exactly invite those kids on the field. What do you do with seven- and eight-year-old kids who look up at you and ask you for your autograph?

Two days later, on August 30, I began hitting the ball more solidly than I had at any other time that year. I was really stinging the ball. I was getting hits, and even when I made out, I'd hit the ball hard at somebody. I ran up a sixteen-game hitting streak, the longest one on the ballclub in 1969, and from August 31 to the end of the year raised my average from .242 to .255. It must have been the feeling that I'd made it. It wasn't as if I suddenly saw the ball any better; I guess I just felt better and looser. I hit my nineteenth homer on September 8 against the Indians. Now I knew I had one more goal. Number twenty.

I got it, but not even I could have predicted how it would come. On September 22, the Red Sox announced they were firing Williams as manager and that Pop would take over the club right away for the rest of the season. The next day, Pop's first as interim manager, I hit number twenty against the Yankees at Fenway, as we won big, 8–3. I guess that capped the season for me. I'd hurt my hand toward the end of the season, so I sat out some games, while Billy, back from the minors, got to play in my place and show what he could do. We ended the season in Washington, barely holding the Senators off from taking third place from us, and Rico got his fortieth homer to set a record for an American League shortstop.

That number forty was a tough one for Rico. He just couldn't seem to get it. Rico was pressing and the season was coming to an end. It was time to do something. Rico grabbed his bat out of the rack. You could see that he was tensing up. "Hey, Rico," I called, "Give it to me for a minute." "What do you want it for?" he said. "I'm going to rub in number forty," I said. I took that bat and went down the steps leading to the clubhouse. I reached in under my shirt and pulled out my medal. I tapped the medal on the bat a couple of times. Our clubhouse man, Vinnie Orlando, was standing there watching. "Vinnie," I said. "This will get Rico his fortieth." Then I handed the bat back to Rico and watched as he stepped out into the on-deck circle. He only had this game and one more to hit number forty. Everyone on the bench was rooting for him because he is the kind of team man that we all like. Rico went up to hit. He ran the count to three and one, and hit the next pitch out toward the left-field fence. Frank Howard leaped up, but the ball dropped behind him into the Washington bullpen for a home run. You would have thought we had just won the pennant the way everyone jumped around. I looked over at Vinnie Orlando. His mouth had dropped open about down to his kneecaps. He just stood there and stared at me.

One night in spring training I was out to dinner with Ken Harrelson. Ken gave me a piece of paper and asked me to put down what I thought would be a good year for me. He told me he had already put down what he thought would be a good year for me and he wanted to compare his with mine.

I wrote down what I'd gladly settle for in my comeback year. But before showing him mine, I asked him to let me see his list. It read: A .265 batting average, 25 home runs and 85 RBI's. "I'll take it," I said. Then I showed him mine. It read: A .250 batting average, 20 home runs and 80 RBI's. I thought about this the day the season ended. Ken's was beautiful, but mine was closer. I had hit .255 with 20 homers and 82 RBI's.

That didn't mean I was satisfied. I felt that if I could do that in my first year back that anything was possible. I feel I should be able to hit 30 homers this year, but the thing I want to do the most is knock in 100 runs. But I'd have to hit fourth to have a shot at it. All of a sudden I could see that my father was right—again. I didn't want to retire from baseball. The good month I had in September had something to do with it, of course, and when the Red Sox fired Dick Williams and hired Eddie Kasko, that was icing on the cake. I loved Eddie Kasko before I even met him; anybody who replaces Dick Williams I'm in love with.

During the winter I met Kasko a few times and I liked him. He's quiet, conservative, and warm. Right from the start, he told me he was going to bat me fourth in 1970, and any talk about trading Yaz or me or any of the other regulars was immediately dropped when he was hired. We needed pitching and maybe Gary Peters, who we got from the White Sox, would help. I also felt that Billy was going to make us a stronger club in 1970. He played most of last year for Kasko at Louisville, where he batted .298 and had 13 homers and 81 runs-batted-in. He's told me how much he liked Kasko and I've always felt Billy was a pretty good judge of character.

Billy is a lot different than I am. My brother Richie and I are more alike. Billy is always on the move, he can't sit still. I don't mind taking a nap once in a while, but Billy doesn't have the time. For one thing, he's terribly interested in astronomy. He's read so many books on UFO's he's convinced himself there are flying saucers. He spent $500 on a telescope a few years ago and set it up in the backyard at Swampscott. He'd stay out there for hours at a time just looking at the moon. That's not my kick at all. Richie and I would yell out to him to give the thing a rest. But Billy would tell us to come out and "Have a look at this." So I'd go out and look through the lens and I saw the moon with all those craters over it. It was beautiful to see, but after one minute I saw enough craters to last me the rest of my life. My father calls Billy the mad scientist. That's because Billy likes to fix things. He likes to take things apart to see what makes them work. The only trouble is he can't put them together again. He's ruined every single radio I've ever owned.

Billy is more shy than I am. But he makes out with the girls pretty well. Maybe not as well as I do, but he's a close second. As a matter of fact, I think he's trying to take the lead. Last year, his first in the majors, he started going after some of my girls. This is something I'm very serious about. One of the big reasons my roommate, Tony Athanas, and I get along so well is that we have agreed never to take out the same girl.

But Billy and his friends see nothing wrong with dating the same girl, unless there's something serious going on. I was out driving one day and pulled up to a light. I looked out of my car and there was Billy in his car sitting with a girl, Cheryl, I had dated. He knew I had taken her out. When he saw me he turned the same color as his car—a sickly green. Then he waved, the light changed, and we both drove off.

The next night we were both at the house in Swampscott and

I told him my feelings on the subject. "There are a million girls in this town," I said. "Why do you have to go out with the same one I take out?"

"What's wrong with that?" he said. "You've only been out with her once or twice, and you haven't seen her in a couple of months."

My parents were sitting in the next room watching TV and I yelled in there to ask them to come in and referee this thing between Billy and me. "I want to know if I'm right or wrong," I said. "If I'm wrong, tell me." They listened to both of us, and when we were through my mother said Billy was right and my father said I was right: a draw. Richie was just sitting there in a corner listening to every word, but not saying anything.

Billy finally said, "All right, I'm not going to take anybody out that you go out with anymore. Is that all right?"

Now I simmered down and said, "Ah, it doesn't really matter. It just bothered me when I saw the two of you yesterday. Let's forget about it."

Billy said, "Well, I guess you're right."

Two weeks later, I was sneaking out of Fenway Park. I had on my straw hat, a phony mustache, and sunglasses. I was walking over the bridge toward my apartment when I suddenly spotted Cheryl walking hand in hand with Richie. They didn't recognize me with that outfit on, and I fell in behind them and followed them. Suddenly, I stopped myself and said, "This is ridiculous." I stood there for about a minute and said to myself, "Oh, boy, my father's next." Then I started laughing and people must have thought I was nuts standing there like that and laughing. Not till months later did I bring the subject up with Richie, and he blushed when I told him about it. I've got a feeling that Richie does better than Billy and me combined.

While I feel very close to Billy it has always been hard for me to show it. We never go out together and while he has never said anything about it to me, I know this bothers him. I know he'd like to be closer to me, but I have always found it hard. I guess I never believed that brothers should do things together. Maybe it's because of something that happened to us in spring training in 1969. It was Billy's first year with the club. He and I went to a place and sat down at the bar. Billy went off to make a phone call. When Billy came back we noticed this guy had taken his seat at the bar. The guy told Billy to get lost. I could see something starting and before it did I got off my stool, grabbed the guy and told him if he laid a hand on Billy I'd mess him up pretty good. He could see how angry I was and he took off. I guess I realized for the first time that when I'm out with Billy it makes me overprotective.

There isn't anything I wouldn't do for Billy, or Richie, or my parents. I love them all so much I wouldn't do anything that would make them ashamed of me. For example, I would never smoke pot or get involved with drugs in any way. If I ever did and my brothers found out about it I'd lose face and faith with them. I'd never want that to happen. Besides, my life has really been beautiful and I don't need any help from drugs.

I remember in my second year in the big leagues I was out with this girl in Detroit. I had just picked her up at a club and we were driving around. We passed a certain neighborhood and she suddenly ducked down in her seat so she couldn't be seen from the outside. I asked her why she had done that and she told me she didn't want to be recognized around there; she was the girl friend of some big Mafia leader.

Well, I didn't want any part of that and I told her she should have told me she had a boy friend because then I wouldn't have asked her out. But she said she wanted to be out with me. I quickly tried to get out of that area. We got on an expressway and I was looking as hard as I could to find someplace to drop her off. I was sort of half-paying attention to her when I suddenly noticed she had gone into her handbag and pulled out a syringe. She took off her scarf and tied it around her arm and then stuck the syringe in her arm.

That did it. I pulled over to the side of the road, got out of the car on my side, went around to her side and pulled her out. That's where I left her. That's the closest I ever got to drugs and I don't ever want to get any closer. I feel sorry for the kids who get mixed up with that stuff. I think they're only hiding from themselves and their troubles.

My life with women has been confusing to me because I think not wanting to settle down has ruined my relationship with a lot of beautiful people. Sometimes I've been cold when I became too close to someone. I didn't know how to handle the situation, so the best thing I could think of doing was to move on. I made up my mind not to get married until I got my complete fling out of life. I want to go out with every kind of woman, old and young, tall and short. I guess you can say I'm experimenting.

Marriage scares me. Right now I can't imagine living with one person for the rest of my life. I'm very moody. I like quiet. Any girl who marries me would have to understand this, and she would also have to be completely mine. I mean no career, no nothing: just me. That's a hard kind of girl to go looking for. I often feel I'm going to wind up with some farm girl—some beautiful farm girl—because big-city girls have too many other things on their minds.

The older I've grown the more selective I've become. When I

234

was younger all I wanted was fun, sex, and a little companionship. Now I've changed. When I date a girl, I mentally examine her and ask myself, can I live with this girl for the rest of my life. I know what I want in a wife now, and if I can't find these qualities, I just won't get married. Marriage is very important to me. I can't wait for the day I hold my child.

When I look back at some of the girls I've known, I realize I was too harsh with them. I let little things bother me, and I guess I made the mistake of forgetting about girls who were great to be with because I was afraid to let them get too close to me. But I never wanted to hurt anyone by picking up and moving out, so I always let them know I wasn't ready to settle down. So sex became too important. I didn't want to get into anyone's mind; I wasn't ready for a mental hangup.

When I was still in high school, I met Julie Makarkis. She's the girl I got into that fight over when I broke my thumb. Julie had and still has all the qualities I like in a girl. She's honest, kind and sincere; she's never said a bad word about anyone. I first met her in the library in Lynn when I was seventeen, and we went steady for two and a half years. I liked her so much that when I was nineteen, I even gave her a hope chest.

At the time everyone was telling me not to get married, even those people who were happily married. I heard it so many times I got scared. I realized I was too young to settle down, but how was I going to tell this to Julie? I didn't want to hurt her or her family, with whom she was very close. I'd never been so close to anyone before, but still I knew I had to make the move.

Shortly after the 1964 season started, I decided to tell Julie I wanted to break up. I drove over to her house one night and we went out. I didn't say very much. I couldn't, because I was trying to figure out what I was going to say to her. About eleven o'clock, I took her home and we stopped to talk in her hallway downstairs.

She was very nervous, so I guess she suspected what was on my mind. Over and over again, I kept thinking about all the beautiful things we'd done together. But I felt we were not mature enough to settle down.

"Julie," I said, "I think it's best for us to break up. If we really love each other, we'll come back to each other. But right now I think you ought to go out with a lot of other guys."

She said she didn't want to go out with anyone else, and then she started crying. I couldn't take that; my stomach knotted up and I begged her to stop crying. I really don't know how I didn't cry, too. I told her I wanted to date other girls and find out more of what life was all about. Rather than prolonging the scene, I just said, "Good-bye," and walked out to my car. I could hear her crying and calling me. I wanted to go back, but something kept me from giving in.

For several nights after that, I stared at the phone in my house and thought about calling her back. But I couldn't do it. I know some people thought I had broken off with Julie because I had made it to the big leagues. But that wasn't so. I broke it up then for the same reason I'm still single now. I haven't had enough running around yet. I hated to think about being married at only nineteen.

When I get married I hope to never cheat on my wife. I guess this sounds corny to a lot of people, but I'm going to get all my fling over with. I don't care if it takes me another ten years before I settle down for good. But I hope to have a tight family held together by prayer, love, and respect.

It's really a good thing for me I haven't married anybody yet.

At twenty-five, I can't say my life has had any kind of game plan. I've lived from minute to minute; the only stop came when that ball hit me in the head. That gave me time to think and maybe it's helped me to find some answers. But changing isn't an easy process and I know it's going to take me some more time. I just hope I'm on the right track now.

One of the things I tried to do last winter was to get myself into some legitimate businesses, both for the off-seasons to come and for the day when I can't play baseball anymore. I have started an employment agency called Tony C.'s Girls, Inc., which I think is going to be a big thing. I have always wanted to do TV commercials, but always seemed to go about it in the wrong way. Now I think I'm with an outfit that will make it possible. And I have a few other things I am looking into for the future.

When I was very young my dad told me I was going to find very few true friends in life, but when I did to be grateful and hang on to them. I don't have many friends, but I guess the guy I'm closest to is my roommate, Tony Athanas, Jr. He's a couple of years older than I am and he manages restaurants for his father around Boston. Tony's father runs Anthony's Pier 4, one of the world's great eating places, and Tony manages two others called Anthony's Hawthorne, in Lynn, and the General Glover, in Swampscott. I'm also close to Bill and Donna Bates, who live near us in Brookline. Bill is the trainer for the Boston Patriots football team and is the only guy in the world who can make me laugh any time he wants.

If I've learned anything in twenty-five years of living, I hope it's how to get along better with people. It's difficult to be nice to everyone all the time when you're a ballplayer, and I know I've made people mad on occasion. But the pressures are always there and a lot of things make the papers which aren't always correct.

Still, baseball is my number-one interest, no matter what else you might read. The biggest thing that happened to me over the winter was being named The Comeback of the Year. Then in Pittsburgh last February, I received the Fred Hutchinson award for courage at the Dapper Dan dinner. I spent the winter getting in the best shape of my life. I enrolled in a karate school in Somerville and took private instruction. But it wasn't so I could become a killer. Karate quickens you and makes you stronger. I swung a weighted bat 500 times every day till my hands blistered, then took a week off in Puerto Rico before reporting to Winter Haven. If I don't have the best year of my career in 1970, I don't know when I will.

I thank God for my parents. I love them. I more than love them; without them I am nothing. Having them behind me has been the most important thing in my life. I often wonder what it will be like when they die. I know they will someday, but I hope they will both live to be 150. There is no way of hiding from death. Me, I want to live till I'm 104 and play five more years after that.

From all the things that have happened to me, I have to feel I'm some sort of special guy. I really can't understand why I can't see well enough to read for any length of time, but when I go up to the plate I can see the ball. It has to be a miracle. The support so many people have given me was necessary, but I think God made it possible. Which is why I say I must be a special kind of guy. God has always been good to my family, but this time I think He went out of his way.